REASONS THEATER LEISURE MAY

INFLUENCE COUNTRIES DEVELOPMENT

JOHN LOK

Contents

Preface

Introduction

What are the different unique characteristics between one developing country and one developed country ? How to judge whether the country had been either developed or had been developing ? What factors influence the country development speed? In my this book, I shall indicate New Zealand whether is one developed country or developing country, although its farming industry , e.g. sheep cloth manufacturing, breef and pork meat food export industries had developed long time, but what weaknesses, it owns to influence its continue development easily as well as what strengths it lacks to influence New Zealand is still staying in the developing stage in possible in global leading position. What factors influence US, UK their technological development can not be continued innovated to cause worse development to compare Germany 's heavy manufacturing industry future development in possible.

Nowadays, on movie and opera art performance lesiure market, our leisures businesses have many different kinds to let consumer individual choice, for example, movie, opera art management, football performance, swimming , bicycle competition performance etc. indoor leisure activities. How can persuade audiences to buy ticket to see any one of these indoor leisure performance? We need to learn audience psychological factor and indoor environment factor if leisure businessmen hope to increase their audience number easily. Why and how theater leisure may influence countries continue develop?

Prologue

Table Of Content

Why and how developed countries need
assist developing countries to develop

- Global resource is shortage to allocate unfair challenge p.66-70
- Some developed countries have obligation to help developing countries
- Rich countries have responsibilites to assist global economy development or balance economy development

Methods developing countries can
become developed countries

- Main industries aspects need to develop p.71-80
- The challenges are needed to solve in development process
- What a developing country should do to be a developed one?
- Developed Countries need to help Developing Countries to increase their competitive effort in societies

Can bring global benefit when all
countries are developed countries

1. How Globalization Affects Developed Countries

Conflicting Globalization Views

- Benefits of globalization
- Drawbacks of globalization
- What Is Globalization?
- Why and how globalization may achieve when global countries can develop to become developed countries ?
- Components of Globalization
- The degree to which an organization is globalized and diversified has bearing on the strategies that it uses to pursue greater development and investment opportunities.

● Effect of globalization on developing countries or third world countries

● What influences to the countries like china and India has grown tremendously after globalization.

● Effect of globalization on developed countries when all developing countries can become developed countries

● Development of "Regional economic" will truly help India to build viable economic future for its citizens.

● Regional economies help to reduce domination of developed economies on the developing economies.

2. Economic growth advantages and disadvantages

● Are economic growth and development worthwhile?

● Economic growth and development of Asia when all or many developing countries can develop to be developed countries

● Model of economy development: The production function how can be influenced to change when many or all developing countries can become developed countries

● How global developed economy influences household expenditure decision?

● How global developed economy influences the labor supply function changes ?

● How global developed economy influences wage rate versus labor leisure changes?

● Economic development theories: Harrod-Domar theory

Will developed countries become
developing countries

● Why does illness can cause global economic recession to developed countries p.81-91

● Increasing social crime rate and government assistance may cause developed countries to become developing coutries

- How can watching theatre benefit the mind?
- What physical benefits can bring to individual from theatre performance?
- Can theatre performance improve studend individual academic performance?
- How do the arts improve academic performance?

Audience choices between theatre and cinema movie leisure

- Supply and demand view to future theatre and cinema movie leisure industry

Movie and opera art performance leisure
consumer psychology

- CINEMA MOVIE AUDIENCE LEISURE PSYCHOLOGY p.146-160
- Why has theatre become such an important art-form?
- THE PSYCHOLOGY OF PERFORMING ARTS:THEATRE AND HUMAN EXPRESSION
- What is the role of spectacle in performing arts?
- Designing a Good Theater to influence audience seeing movie or opera art performance positive emotion feeling factor
- What is theatre's economic role?

CHAPTER I

Defining developed and developing countries differences

- What are the developed countries and developing countries
characteristics

What factors cause the differences between developed countries and developing countries? Do they have significant unique characteristics to be discovered to influence their differences? I shall attempt to indicate evidences to explain whether these are significant different unique characteristics between any developed countries and developed countries as below:

ON economic measurement aspect, low-and middle income economies are usually referred to as developing economies , and the upper middle income and the high income are referred to as developed countries. So, a developing country also called a less developed country or emerging market, it has a lower gross domestic product(GDP) than developed countries, with a less nature and sophisticated economy. The difference is between developed and developing countries. It may indicate that developed countries refer to the Sovereign (independent) nation/ state whose economy has highly progressed and possesses great technological improvement, as compared to other nations.

The countries with low industrialization and low human development indix are formed as developing countries. The World Bank classified the world's economies into four groups, based on Gross National Income per capita: high, upper middle, lower-middle , and low income countries. Least developed countries, landlocked developing countries and small island developing states are all sub-groupings of developing countries. However, it is not ensure that it is only all islands are developing countries, e.g. New Zealand may be one developing country or low developed country also. Experts have said the Guyana has one of the fastest -growing economies in the world.

The unique characteristics differences between developed countries and developing countries. They may include: developing countries are ususally poor, according to the Asian development bank, the major causes of poverty may include: Low economic growth, a week agricultural sector, increased population rates and a high volume of inequality. So, the features of developing countries, their common characteristics may include: low per capita real income, low per capita real income is one of the most defining because amony any developed countries , they may also include highly and lowly developed countries. For example, Norway is the most developed nation in the world. Switzerland is the second developed country in the world, Ireland is the third-most developed country. Then all of these nations may be highly developed countries , e.g. Germany, Hong Kong, China, Australia, Iceland, Sweden. So , it seems that New Zealand may be a lowly developed country to compare above these highly developed countries.

- What factors assist the developing countries to become developed countries

However, the most developing countries in the world, they

may include India, Brazil, China, Argentina is actually considered a developing country and characteristics of developing economies, high population is continue growing. Otherwise, China had began to use methods to discourage Chinese families to born more than one child in order to avoid population continue grows to bring social future burden.

Dependence on primary sector, e.g. Africa and India and New Zealand , they were still depending on main agricutural fruit, rice primary farming industry for themselves main GDP export income source as well as dependence on exports of primary commodities. So, developing countries should need focus on human development, it will remain the main focus of developing countriespost 2015 year. In this regard, the transition of developed countries to equitable and sustainable consumption will make in easier for developinf countries to pursue their human development goals in a more environmental susttainable way.

Hence, human development will may to help developing countries to develop more easily. It is future essential element to assist any one developing countries to be developed countries in success.

The unique characteristics of developing countries include that: Literacy rate is quite low as people are deprived of education facilities, the standard of living in developing countries is normally not very high. Otherwise, developed countries literacy rate is quite high , due to better education ayatem and life expectancy rate is more , due to better standing living. So, in general, the standard of living is very high to developed countries, e.g. UK, US , they have many the low income level or poor people still may have enough money to save in bank and the number of poor people is less in themselves countries, due to definitional discrepancies countries, such as Maxico, Greece and Turkey. India may be nowadays developing countries.

However, there are agrument or disagreement between developed and developing countries. The developed countries say that developing countries must stop burning fossil, fuels and other things that harm the atmosphere. Otherwise, developing countries argue that developed countries have developed by burning the fossil fuels. They say their development will be affected if they stop burning fuels. For Japan example, it is one highly developed country because ir is one of the largest and most developed economies in the world. It has a well-educated, industrious workforce and its large , affluent population makes it is one of the world's biggest consumer markets. Otherwisem New Zealand is not high technological and industrious developed country, it still depends on agricultural fruits, meats export farming industry for main GDP growth source. So, comparison New Zealand and Japan development speed, New Zealand is one lowly developed country. Otherwise, Japan is one highly developed country in nowadays our society. But, the comparison between New Zealand and China, China is still a developing country , but New Zealand may be one lowly developed country to compare China because Chinese government has repeatedly stated that China is the world's largest developing country, despite rapid economic growth over the past four decades. However, according to the 2018 survey, the United States is the world's most powerful country, following countries may include: Japan, Israel, South Korea, Saudi, Arabia, but the safest country may be Iceland because its crime rate is the least. Although, US, UK may be highly developed countries, but their crime rate may be high position. So, one highly developed country does not represent that it must have the most safest social living environment to let its citizen to feel safe to live. It may be any one highly developed countries themselves failure points.

However, environmental factors may also stop a country from developing because some places experience environmental issues, which can present them from developing, examples might be extremee flooding or desertification social factors may also stop a country from developing, e.g. high crime rate, high unemployed rate, low safe living feeling rate, low living standard, they are some parts of the world have issues that are caused by people to influence any countries continue to develop to be one developed country easily. So, all of these factors can assist any one developing country to become developed country.

CHAPTER II

What factors cause developed countries continue developed

What factors cause New Zealand to be developed country in success

What factors influence New Zealand is still one lowly developed country? Can New Zealand fight itself country weaknesses to become one highly developed country? I shall attempt to indicate several evidences to explain what factors influence New Zealand can not develop to reach mature social development stage in itself nowadays society are below:

New Zealand is a small population country. It has only 4.8 million . However, there are many NZ people feel poverty to live. The causes of poverty in New Zealand. They may include: income inequality, lack of a simple fund support from government, lack of economic infrastructure, poor access to education, poor access to healthcase, opinion was evenly diviced on the primary cause of child poverty in NZ. Forty percent of NZ people said it was due to economic factors including unemployment, low wages, and rising living costs, the ever-increasing monthly power bills the the NZ government won't regulate or gone down.

However, in NZ, poverty is seen as relative, whereby those suffering deprivation are often struggling to feed their children, living in insecurce circumstances and unable to enjoy a satisfying social life easily to many New Zealanders. As a result, many NZ family members' health suffers and children fail to achieve a sound level of education. IN fact, there is poverty in the midst of prosperity in NZ. There is poverty amidst prosperity: There are around 682,500 people in poverty in this country or one in seven households, including around 220, 000 children .

In general, there are the causes of poverty reasons to any countries, they may include: lack of good jobs / job growth, lack of good education, the second root causes of poverty is a lack of education, a lack of social welfare, weather/ climate change, social injustice, lack of food and water, lack of government support. Although NZ may be belonged to one developed country. But, it is still staying on the lowly developed stage in long time development process. The main factors cause NZ is still one lowly developed country. They may include : lack of good jobs growth in order to let graduates can find good jobs to do and education level can not be improved . What factors cause NZ lacks good job growht and poor education improvement in long time?

In fact, NZ likes many developed countries, its witnessing a transformation in itself economy and employment opportunities. Its traditional exporting sectors , such as dairy, meat, forestry and tourism, remain important drivers of growth. So, NZ's main source of income, they are agricutlural products export, principally meat, dairy products, and fruits and vegetables , crude oil and wood and paper products are also significant. However, the impacts of poverty in NZ, because children in poor communities are three times more likely than the average child to be sick twice as likely to end up in hospital, and sudden unexpected death in infancy rates are more than 6 times higher for infants in the most disadvantaged areas of NZ. These harmful effects run into adulthood in NZ.

What are the most common jobs in NZ? The most popular carre was police officer. SO, when many NZ people hope to seek policeforce jobs. NZ will bring poor job growth development chance to let graduates have plans to develop other professional career in society. Many NZ graduates only consider policeforce jobs, it is one poor social job culture in NZ. However, NZ education is better than America in possible. NZ is definitely superior to the US, in the OECD nations indication, NZ is ranked 3 rd for education quality behinf Finland and Canada, the US ranks about 12 th . Why does NZ still be one lowly developed country in possible, when it can have superior education system?

In fact, NZ ranks highly on most indicators of well-being, but average social level of incomes are low , in general, inequality income were allocated and made NZ economy less developed in the face of shocks, due to low labour productivity factor, low labour productiviey is only partly explained by the farming main industry of the NZ economy and is primarily a consequence of low mulit-factor productivity growth within NZ other industries development, instead of farming industry as well as weak investment on other industries, e.g. technololgical, computer manufacturing , medicine life science drug manufacturing, construction, engineering, e.g. robotic manufacturing etc. different industries development. So, NZ neglects to consider how to develop other industries instead of concentrating on only development on agricultural industry.

However, economic geography is an important factor in NZ's poor productivity performance as the small size and remoteness of the economy diminish its access to global markets, the scale and efficiency of domestic businesses, the level of competition, and the ability to benefit from innovation at the global frontier. All of these many be the

main cause weaknesses to NZ countinue development in success.
Moreover, NZ government lacks good policy to support its productivity growth, e.g. lacking to promoting international connections, none removing barriers to fixed capital investment to NZ domestic any industries development, instead of agricultural industry, accessing benefits of agricultural industry, accessingg benefits by improving urban planninf, enhancing competition and increasing investment in innovation and intangibles.
Hence, poor productivity technological improvement may be on main factor to cause NZ productivity growth is poor. It is main reason to cause NZ is one lowly developed country in long time, because global highly developed countries concerned high technological productivity is expected to be the main driver of income source , in particular via investment in technology and knowledge-based capital. So, any highly developed countries began to believe that economic growth from productivity improvements contributes to welfare through increasing the worker individual income that can be earned from each hour worked, providing individuals with the option to work lesss or consume mocw job and service. Hence , NZ lacks high technological productivity improved to let any one talent NZ person can have chance to use his / her talent knowledge to do high technological jobs in order to attribute NZ society and to earn high hour income. NZ is only developing agricultural industry nowadays. SO, agricultural jobs wil be common jobs in NZ developed country. Hence, low technolgical productive improvement may be main factor to influence NZ to be one lowly developed country in long time.

What factors influence US and UK continue development Why do US and US be a developed country? It has a high-income economy and a very high human development index rating. Ranking 13 th in the world. Today, the UK , US remains one of the world's great powers with considerable economc, cultural , military, scientific, technological and political influence internationally. Why are UK and US econome so strong? It's quality of life is generally considered high, and the economy is quite diversified . The sectors that contibute must be the US, UK 's GDP are services, manufacturing, construction and tourism . Moreover, UK and US are the world's largest economy by normimal GDP and net wealth and they are the second largest by purchasing power. Themselves nations's economy is fueled by natural resources, a well-developed and high productivity.

It seems that UK and US have a mixed economic development, developed through free market and global economy , which are regulated by their governments to prevent market failure easily.

CHAPTER III

What Factors Influence Social Development Speed

What factors cause why some countries can develop rapidly ? What factors cause some countries develop slowly? It would be hard to find a more fundamental conept for the social development and human development. The social development science is about human societies how we develop, so we had better have some idea to explain how and why what factors cause some countries can develop rapidly , e.g. US, UK, or what factors cause some countries can develop slowly, e.g. China, India. The reaons that there has been a question about the development speed to any countries , it has been an active and influential movement to insist that this was a human social development question. Why does Inida has many years history, otherwise, US has less many years histroy, what factors influence US can develop more rapidly to compare Inida? Even, India seems to be one developing country in nowadays society.

From sociobiology to social development psychology

What factors to India is facing to influence it can not succeed to develop to be highly developed country easily? Human cognitive mechanisms evolved in the Pleistocene, the period from about 2 million years ago, about 10,000 years ago, the end of the last Ice age, MOtivating this choice is the thought that substantial periods of development time are required for significant evoluntionary change, such as social need change, family need change, country need change. Much of Evolutinnary psychology has consisted of reflection on the different countries changing conditions that might have obtained during this perios, and the human development behaviors what would have been most favoured by natural selection given those conditions.

First of all to what influences human feels we need to develop, a lot of human behavior has roots that are far more ancient. Sociability , for instance, is not a uniquely human attribute. But significant changes in the nature of human sociality are evident over historical periods of tens or hundrends of years, presumably because they are due to cultural improvement, or raising human cultural quality , so our cultural improvement psychology influences why some countries can not develop rapidly, such as India does not consider itself Indian cultural level needs to raise significantly. Otherwise, US condiers itself American cultural level need to raise significantly. So, this cultural development reason may explain why India is still one developing country, although, its has many years history to compare US.

Social Development Psychology

Another important point about social development issus, it is the environmental factor, it is one picture to influence why some countries develop rapidly , but some countries still develop slowly. I don nor need to pursue that argument , since the focus will remain on the human development case, and no one could suppose that the social enviroment that human create for, among the other things, the production of new human social behaviors, is simply a consequence of genetically determined human behavior. For example, American hopes that it can create many talent people to help itself country to develop, so talent people development environment need can influence US can have many talent people to create to help itself country to develop to be highly developed country in short time, e..g. space science, life science etc.

I wished to emphasize particularly the ability of cultural evolution to transform the social development history to different countries issus. It seems clear that humans have learned in quite recent time to construct a remarkably social changing environment for the development for their young. So, any countries their future development, they must depend on how many talent young people, they can create. It is very important issue to influence any one country to develop to be one high developed or low developed or developing country. For that reason their introduction should be seen as representing major cultural improvemernt and social environment factors to influence any countries their future development speed. For this simple example, many further illustrate the point, they indicate that the mobile phone did not exist when I was a child. In fact, it is for hardly more than a decade that it has been for everyday life in developed countries. Ans whereas it may seem only more or less need for people of my generation, for those aged, say 10 to 20 , age, it is as unthinkable to deprived of one's phone as to wander the streets stark naked. Most teenagers move through the would, when this smart phone technological development, it can influence any one feels that it is essential product to our daily need. It is one cultural improvement factor example , it can explain why global many people feel smart phones are essential product to satisfy us need. It is not, therefore, merely behavior that has changed for those who have grown up with the mobile phone, but the social environment can bring indirect to influence any one , even old age feels smart phone need, when old age people can contact many young people , they must own least one smart phone for personal use. So, cultural improvement and social environment changing need both factors can influence any one country may make development decision in short time or long time, when the country people feel that they have urgent social and cultural improvement changing need rapidly.

CHAPTER IV

What are the differences between developing and developed countries

I shall explain the difference between developed and developing countries characteristics as below:
Countries are divided into two major categories by the United Nations, which are developed countries and developing countries. The classification of countries is based on the economic status such as GDP, GNP, per capita income, industrialization, the standard of living, etc. Developed Countries refers to the soverign state, whose economy has highly progressed and possesses great technological infrastructure, as compared to other nations. The countries with low industrialization and low human development index are termed as developing countries. Developed Countries provides free, healthy and secured atmosphere to live whereas developing countries, lacks these things.
The characteristics between developing and developed countries may include as below:
Developed countries means that a country having an effective rate of industrialization and individual income is known as Developed Country. Otherwise, developing Country is a country which has a slow rate of industrialization and low per capita income. Developed countries have low unemployment and poverty, developing countries have usually high unemployment and poverty. developed countries have low infant mortality rate, death

rate and birth rate is low while the life expectancy rate is high. Otherwise, developing countries have high infant mortality rate, death rate and birth rate, along with low life expectancy rate. Developed countries have better living conditions and high standard of living, but developing countries have bad living conditions and low standard of living. Developing countries have high GDP from industrial sector income source, otherwise, developed countries have high GDP income from service sector income source. Developing countries have high industrial growth. Otherwise, developed countries, they rely on the developed countries for their growth. Developed countries have high equal of distribution of income, otherwise, developing countries have high unequal of distribution of income. Finally, developed countries have effectively utilized to factors of production, otherwise, developing countries have ineffectively utilized to factors of production. Overall , any thing of developed countries are better than developing countries in nowadays societies.

Between developed and developing countries, one can identify a variety of differences. This differentiation of countries, as developed and developing, is used to classify countries according to their economic status based on per capita income, industrialization, literacy rate, living standards, etc.

● What are Developed Countries?

They have usually these similar characteristics as below:

(1) Developed countries have industrial growth and enjoy flourishing economy. Developed countries experience marked development and growth in the areas such as transportation, business, and education. Developed countries are characterized by a low death rate and low birth rate as well. There is usually a very small gap between

the two rates in developed countries.

(2) Developed countries are not characterized by shortcomings. They are well-developed in all fronts and are served well by water supplies, amenities, educational institutions, health care concerns. This is because of the fact that people are endowed with awareness about every possible aspect relating to human existence. The absence of shortcomings in the developed countries is possibly due to the fact there is a low birth rate in these countries. Nutrition is available in plenty to mothers and infants in developed countries.

- What are Developing Countries?

They have usually these similar characteristics as below:

(1) Developing countries depend on the developed countries for help to establish their industries. They have only begun to taste the growth of the economy. Developing countries are in the beginning stages of development in the areas of education, business, and transportation.

(2) Developing countries are characterized by many shortcomings. These shortcomings include less awareness regarding matters relating to health, poor amenities, shortage in water supply, shortcoming in the area of medical supply, a higher rate of birth rate. The most important and worrying factor in the developing countries is the factor of poor nutrition. Poor nutrition to both mothers and infants is the main concern in the developing countries. Due to high birth rates, the probability of natural diseases is more in developing countries. Hence, the death rates are also eventually high in developing countries. However, since natural diseases increase by high rates in the developing countries, they will have a short population doubling time. In the case of developing countries, there is usually a big gap between the birth rate and the death rate.

Infant mortality factor is influenced by the development factor of countries. A developing country for that matter would have higher infant mortality than a developed country.

Overall, economists will differ their different characteristcs from these several aspects as below:

Developed countries display a high level of development. Developing countries: Developing countries display a lower development in different areas such as industrialization, human capital, etc. Developed countries have industrial growth. Developing countries depend on the developed countries for help to establish their industries. Developed countries enjoy flourishing economy. Developing countries begin to taste the growth of the economy. Developed countries experience marked development and growth in the areas such as transportation, business, and education. Developing countries are in the beginning stages of development in the areas of education, business, and transportation. Developed countries are characterized by a low death rate and low birth rate as well. There is usually a very small gap between the two rates in developed countries. In developing countries there is usually a big gap between the birth rate and the death rate. Hence, in overall, any aspects are worse, slow growth to developing countries compare to developed countries.

- What are general their GDP difference

Developed Countries:

A developed nation is one that has a very high rank in industrial advancement, constructs its economy in light of innovation and assembling rather than agribusiness. The variables of production, for example, human and regular assets are completely used bringing about an increment underway and utilization which prompts a very high rank in per capita salary. A nation with a more Human Development Index (HDI) is viewed as a developed nation. It not just measures the financial improvement and GDP of a nation additionally its instruction and future.

Developing Countries:

A developing nation is those having a way of life or level of modern advancements well beneath that conceivable with money related or specialized guide; a nation that is not yet exceptionally industrialized. A country having less utilization of resources and low income per capita which leads to low GDP of a country.

- Developed VS Developing Countries will have different development or growth speed to compare as below:

?Industrial Economies:

In developed countries, economy depends on industrial sector instead of agriculture sector. There is more development in industrial sector. In developing countries, mostly economy depends on agriculture sector and they are moving toward industrialization.

?Citizens:

In developed countries, citizens and well off and rich. In developing countries, proportion of rich citizens is very low.

?Unemployment:

In developed countries, there is no such issue of unemployment. They provide many employment opportunities to the citizens. In developing countries, issue of unemployment is there and it affects the economy of country very badly.

?Education:

The growth rate in education sector is very high in developed countries and they have best education systems. Whereas the growth rate of developing countries in education sector is low as compare to developed countries. While developing countries are following the education system of developed countries to achieve the standard.

?Technological advantages:

In developed countries, every place is full with technological advancements and they always try to make it better. In developing countries, there are many undeveloped rural areas and even urban sector have less technological advancements.

?Roads:

Developed countries have a very sound infrastructure by having better roads, railway tracks, airports etc. Developing countries don't have a sound infrastructure as compare to developed countries.

?Government:

There exists stable government in developed countries so that they make effective and reliable policies for better economic development. Developing countries have unstable governments and mostly try to following the policies made by developed countries.

?Health care:

In developed countries, good and better facilities for health have been provided to citizens. In developing countries, health care facilities are not so good and acceptable.

?Resources:

In developed countries, the natural and human resources are fully and efficiently consumed. In developing countries, many of the natural resources are still untouched and others resources are also not fully utilized.

?Income:

There is a high level of income as per citizen living in developed country so that they have high GDP and GNP. Developing countries have low level of income as per citizen living in country with unequal distribution of income as that have low GDP and GNP.

?High Human Development Index (HDI):

In developed countries, there are best education systems and better health care and high income level so this leads to high value and ranking of HDI. In developing countries, there are low income level and fewer facilities for health care and low rates of education so this leads to low or middle ranking in HDI.

?Life expectancy:

In developed countries, due to better health care the life expectancy has been increased and they have low birth rates as well as low death rates. In developing countries, life expectancy is not so high but has high rates of birth and death due to less facilities and education.

?Water and food supply:

In developed countries, safe and clean water is supplied with plentiful supply of food items and good housing condition. In developing countries, dirty and unsafe water is supplied with less reliable food items and poor condition of houses.

In conclusion, all our daily necessary need and social need to developing countries growth will be worse to compare developed countries in our nowadays societies.

● How to measure the difference between developed and developing countries ?

The measurement factors between developed and developing countries may include as below:

(1) GDP factor

The classification of a country does not only depend on its income but also on other factors that affect how their citizens live, how their economies are integrated into the global system, and the expansion and diversification of their export industries. A developed country is one that has a high level of industrial development, bases its economy on technology and manufacturing instead of agriculture. The factors of production such as human and natural resources are fully utilized resulting in an increase in production and consumption which leads to a high level of per capita income. A country with a high Human Development Index (HDI) rating is considered a developed country. It not only measures the economic development and GDP of a country but also its education and life expectancy. A developed country's citizens enjoy a free and healthy existence.

(2) Industralization or Commercial aspect factor

The term "developed country" is synonymous to "industrialized country, post-industrial country, more developed country, advanced country, and first-world country." The United Kingdom, France, Germany, Canada, Japan, Switzerland, and the United States of America are only a few of those considered as developed countries. A developing country, on the other hand, is one that has a low level of industrialization.

It has a higher level of birth and death rates than developed countries. Its infant mortality rate is also high due to poor nutrition, shortage of medical services, and little knowledge on health. The citizens of developing countries have a low to medium standard of living because their per capita income is still developing, and their technological capacity is still being developed. There is also an unequal distribution of income in developing countries, and their factors of production are not fully utilized. Developing countries are also referred to as third-world countries or least-developed countries.

Countries are categorized according to their economic

development. The United Nations classifies countries as developed, developing, newly industrialized or developed, and countries in transition such as Kazakhstan, Kyrgyztan, Turkmenistan, and the former USSR. The World Bank classifies countries according to their GNI per capita income: low income ($995 or less) and lower middle income ($996-$3,945); as developing countries with an upper middle income ($3,946-$12,195); and high income (above $11,906) as developed countries.

(3) The country citizen living of standard level

The classification of a country does not only depend on its income but also on other factors that affect how their citizens live, how their economies are integrated into the global system, and the expansion and diversification of their export industries. A developed country is one that has a high level of industrial development, bases its economy on technology and manufacturing instead of agriculture. The factors of production such as human and natural resources are fully utilized resulting in an increase in production and consumption which leads to a high level of per capita income. A country with a high Human Development Index (HDI) rating is considered a developed country. It not only measures the economic development and GDP of a country but also its education and life expectancy. A developed country's citizens enjoy a free and healthy existence.

The term "developed country" is synonymous to "industrialized country, post-industrial country, more developed country, advanced country, and first-world country." The United Kingdom, France, Germany, Canada, Japan, Switzerland, and the United States of America are only a few of those considered as developed countries.

A developing country, on the other hand, is one that has a

low level of industrialization. It has a higher level of birth and death rates than developed countries. Its infant mortality rate is also high due to poor nutrition, shortage of medical services, and little knowledge on health. The citizens of developing countries have a low to medium standard of living because their per capita income is still developing, and their technological capacity is still being developed. There is also an unequal distribution of income in developing countries, and their factors of production are not fully utilized. Developing countries are also referred to as third-world countries or least-developed countries.

In conclusion, the measurement factors to decide whether the country is either developing or developed country. The factors depend on whether: whether the developed country is a country that has a high level of industrialization and per capita income while a developing country is a country that is still in the early stages of industrial development and has a low per capita income , whether the citizens of a developed country enjoy a free, healthy, and affluent existence while citizens of developing countries do not, whether the developed countries are also known as industrialized, advanced, and first-world countries while developing countries are also known as underdeveloped, least developed, and third-world countries. For example, The United States of America, Canada, Switzerland, Belgium, and France are examples of developed countries while India, Malawi, Honduras, the Philippines, and Rwanda are examples of developing countries as well as the infant mortality, birth, and death rates of developing countries are also higher compared to that of developed countries.

Why and how developed countries need
assist developing countries to develop

I think that we should help developing nations, But only to an extent. If we keep, And keep on giving them needs they will start to rely on foreign aid. I think charities are enough, But if the developing countries really need help then we give them help. But not too much, Basically they need to do something themselves and stop relying and take their own action. In exchange for our help maybe they could give us a bit of natural resources? Developing countries may need to be assisted, They may include these reasons:

● Global resource is shortage to allocate unfair challenge

Nowadays, global resources are not equally distributed in different countries. Thus, there are those who belong to the developed nations while there are others that belong to developing countries. With these unequal distribution, it is significant that developed countries must do their part in helping those who belong to the underprivileged sector. It is true that rich countries have their own problems to worry with; Can we introduce aquaponics in developing countries when they don't have the resources that first world countries have? In many areas, there is no electricity available that is needed for many aquaponics systems; developing countries require simplicity, reliability, and freedom from the need of grid powerhowever, it is still their responsibility to help the developing countries people need to solve resource can not be allocated fair problem, such as Afria is one developing country, many people are drinking drink water, due to drought , so they will not feel health and they will feel sick , even die. It is one example of natural resource of clean water shortage challenge to Afica. So, developed country, e.g. US , it has responsibilty to help African to drink clean water because clean water is allocated to supply to America people to drink in preference, due to global clean water supply is decreasing, but human number is increasing and clean water demand will also increase. If clean water is only supplied to US people to drink , even other developed countries people , they can drink the most clean water. The reason is because Africa people is poor or dirty or low education level or it is one developing country etc. factors to influence many African can not often drink any clean water. It is very unfair to this developing country.

In 2010, there were 925 million hungry people in the world; 19 million in developed countries, 37 million in Near East and North Africa, 53 million in Latin America and the Caribbean, 239 Million in Sub-Saharan Africa, and 578 million in Asia and the Pacific. This means that approximately 1 in 7 people are hungry. Protein- energy malnutrition is the most lethal form of malnutrition/ hunger. It is a lack of calories and protein; protein is necessary for key bodily functions including provision of essential amino acids and the development and maintenance of muscles. Bringing aquaponics into third world countries would help prevent this problem by providing fish as a main source of protein. Poor nutrition is the cause or partial cause for at least half of the 10.9 million child deaths each year.

The number of hungry people has increased since 1997 due to three main problems: 1) neglect of agriculture relevant to very poor people by governments and international agencies; 2) worldwide economic crisis and 3) increase in food prices. Children who are poorly nourished suffer up to 160 days of illness each year. Malnutrition affects about 32% of children in developing countries. More than 70% of malnourished children live in Asia. Undernourished pregnant women in developing countries leads to 1 out of

6 infants born with low birth weight; this means higher neonatal death rates, increased occurrences of learning disabilities, mental retardation, poor health, blindness, and premature death. There is enough food to provide everyone in the world with 2, 720 kilocalories per person per day, however many people don't have the land to grow or the money to buy the food they need for themselves and their children. 1 out of 3 people in developing countries are affected by vitamin and mineral deficiency.

So, I feel that aid has diverse results. It can both harm as well help development. Rich countries might be sidetracked in terms of focusing on programs that will spur development. Asian and African nations should create long-term plans that will reduce the dependency on aid, while rich countries should transition from traditional methods of giving support in new ways. Rich countries still argue on the premise that they cannot afford aid or that they are being over-generous. The main idea here is not that they are questioning the aid itself, but the development project. Rich countries must be on the poor countries aid as these people from poor nations face injustice and hardships that are often caused or increased by the programs and decision of rich nations themselves.

However, giving aid is not really an act of generosity. Aid purchases things that donors desire. These might include political support in exchange for the "goodies" that the donor has provided. Rich countries must show support to the poor by abiding on the social, environmental aspects. It can also include adapting to climate change by changing one's own consumption. Another is to accept fairer trade rules. Moreover, rich countries can show true generosity by undergoing changes in the manner of living for the past few decades. It would be fair that rich countries believe they are being generous when they give out dole outs or loose change when poor people around the globe are trying to live on a few basics while living under the system that rich countries have developed. It is a reality that there are also poor people in rich countries that are undergoing tough times. However, it is not ethical to withdraw support from people abroad who are more underprivileged just because there are poor people in rich countries that need help as well.

In fact, many argue that the poor countries that rich countries provide financial aid are doing better economically. It is possible that these countries are growing and catching up with the standard of living. Say for example, the annual income of India might have greatly improved. However, when one divides that with the whole population, each Indian just obtains $3 or less per day. This issue requires obtaining the correct facts not only on financial aid, but on the act of generosity in this world. Rich countries do have a responsibility of giving to those developing country people's living need because they can enjoy any benefits in preference when resource is shortage and global need is also increasing in nowadays societies.

● Some developed countries have obligation to help developing countries

The rich have an obligation to help poor countries who were exploited by their colonial rulers. The United States had a head start with its vast natural resources. But many countries in Europe, such as Britain, became rich due to their colonial reign in Asia. They expanded their empire to include poor, resource-rich nations in Asia. They exploited the region's cheap labour, with workers getting little in return for their hard work. For Hong Kong , developing country and UK developed country. UK had obligation to

help this developing country, HK before 1997.
Hong Kong was different though. Britain ruled Hong Kong for more than 150 years and I think both sides benefited. Today, the city is an international financial centre with a strong economy. But some countries did not benefit from colonial rule. For another example, IBM founder , Bill and Melinda Gates set up the Gates Foundation to help poor countries. We take a lot of things for granted. This cannot go on. A spirit of give-and-take is essential for world harmony. Developed countries may not be bound by law to help poor nations, but they have the responsibility - and the power - to do so.
However, developed countries should help less developed ones. But whether this is an obligation is a matter for debate. I believe the government of a country should be responsible for the well-being of its people. It is wrong to allow outsiders to influence the development of a country. This could lead to serious problems.
A developed country faces various difficulties when choosing who to help. First, its choice could leave a lot of people unhappy and damage its relationship with other countries. Second, allowing foreigners to have a significant influence on a nation could lead to negative consequences. Some donors do not have the best intentions. They could use their power for their own advantage. This could lead to corruption and financial loss in the less developed country. Third, a developing nation may become dependent on foreign aid. And some donors might charge a hefty interest for their financial assistance. This could pose a bigger headache than not receiving aid at all. Hence, rich countries have to be careful when helping poor nations. It involves a lot of politics so the rich have the right to choose the recipient and ensure the aid does not get into the wrong

hands.

● Rich countries have responsibilites to assist global economy development or balance economy development

When global economy is unbalance developing. It will bring the damage of kindly cooperation relationship , e.g. export and import business activities to develop our global economy in success. For example, China and America themselve trade war will cause these both countries' GDP export and import income loss, even global economy will be recession. So, rich country, such as US has responsibility to assist developing country, such as Afria, China, Korea, Taiwan to help them to raise business competive effort and bring long term export and import business cooperation and create many factory jobs to China, Korea, Africa, Taiwan factory workers. Then, they can build kindly business cooperative relationship to bring global economy benefit in long term. Then, our global economy development will succeed more easily.

The first rational basis behind donating to poor countries is the notion that all men are equal. Some may radically oppose this concept, noting that their countries should solely invest its own efforts to remedy impoverished sectors of the population. Given the spread of poverty and homelessness, some have arrived to the conclusion that aiding other countries is not in our best interest. However, this could not be further from the truth. As member of the human race, we all occupy an equitable status as global citizens, and nothing can detract from this truth. Centralise your focus on the relative needs of your nation disregards the ailing needs of the developing world.

The second consideration simply poses the question of why not? Although wealthier, developed countries are plagued by their own respective incidences of poverty and lack of resources, developing countries suffer greatly, in terms of their accessibility to medical aid, vaccines, clean water, and a number of other amenities that are gravely understated in importance. With this said, we must venture beyond the bounds of our own comfort zones, and aid other countries because we are lavished with such a bounty in resources ourselves. Another indispensable benefit of aiding impoverished countries. Foreign diplomacy can significantly aid the national security of any nation. And providing aid to a poor county can ultimately benefit us, improving our perception in their eyes, a cultivating a certain level of civility and coexistence that breeds peace, instead of war. The fewer enemies that a particular nation has, the better.

The final reason is simple. We should empathize with other human beings. Every day, countless children succumb to curable disease, malaria and a number of other pathogens that could easily be treated with outside aid. Both children and adults are sold into slavery and trafficked around the world. Of course, the lingering issue of starvation is a palpable one that still plagues the world today. With this said, we should uphold a noble standard that permits foreign aid for this very reason. One often hears the argument that it is all very well to preach equity but given the planetary emergency the world faces from the threat of climate change we must set aside the equity principle in the interests of humanity as a whole. This is a wholly specious and self serving argument. It reflects the sense of entitlement to an affluent lifestyle, based on energy intensive production and consumption, while denying the even modest aspirations of people in developing countries. For example, global climate changes to warmth challenge , it can cause developing countries people their health to be poor. In a densely interconnected and globalised world, it will be impossible to maintain islands of prosperity in an ocean of poverty and deprivation. It is not that developing countries are claiming the right to spew as much carbon as possible into the atmosphere without regard to the health of the planet. As the main victims of climate change– the impacts of which they are already suffering – they have a much bigger stake in dealing with this challenge. They are, in fact, doing much more than most developed countries, to adopt energy frugal methods of growth, conserving energy, promoting renewable power and limiting waste within the limits of their own resources.

Why and how developing countries people's poor health issue , it may influence developed countries businessmen income ? I shall indicate Africa , developing example , if African are health, then this country will have many workers to assist or help US businessmen to manufacture many products to sell to different countries in short time. If US businessmen hope to pay the low wage to reduce their long time expenditure, Afrian must need have health to do any hard jobs in factories. If US businessmen only feel Chinese workers can help them to do any low wage jobs in factories, when China have many new businesses develop to pay better wages to employ themselves Chinese workers. Then, many Chinese workers may choose to help themselves China employers to do the factory jobs to replace US employers. So, if US can help many African have health to work, it may bring uncounted long time benefits to US businesses. Hence, such as this case, it explains why rich people need to help developing countries to solve health challenge.

Methods developing countries can
become developed countries

● Main industries aspects need to develop

How can developing countries develop to be developed countries in success? What the difficulties to them , that they will need to solve in this development process ? In today's sophisticated society,people of the developing countries are still fighting for their basic righs such a better healthcare,proper education and a sound source of income.While the governments of the underdeveloped countries are struggling to improve the living standards of their people,I believe that contribution by richer nations should be more in this regard. To begin,all human beings should help each other.Govenments of richer nations can take many steps to improve the living standard of the poorer naions. I shall indicate these aspects that they need to concentrate on solving in order to achieve developed countries in success as below:

(1) Healthcare development

Firstly,in the field of healthcare,developed countries can support he underdeveloped in many ways.They can send their expert doctors to train the medical staff in the developing countries.Also,they can open free medical camps in the selected areas of poor countries.In this way free medical advice could be given.Such camps can also start health awarness compaigns to make people aware of unhealthy lifetyle. Moreover, experts from the developed countries can also help with the vaccination programmes in the developing countries.This will led to decrease in infant mortality rate.

(2) Educational development

Secondly,assistance in the field of education should be provide to the poorer nations.The developed countries can provide funds to open new schools and polytechnic institutions.These will not only increase the literacy rate,but will also provide vocational education.Furthermore,the rich governments should provide the students of poor countries an oportunity to study in the prestigious institutions by giving scholarships.This will promote poor people to gain higher education.

(3) Promoting free trade development

Finally,rich nations should help to improve the economy of poor countries.This can be done by promoting free trade.This wil reduce barriers to international trade such as tariff,import quotas and export fee and will help to lift the developing countries out of poverty. To conclude,if we want to live in a beter world with peace and harmony,we should always help each other.Therefore,I believe that richer nations should help the poor countries in all the fields.

- The challenges are needed to solve in development process

During the development process, they developing countries will need to solve these challenges, the developing or underdeveloped countries (as they were earlier named) are poor due to them having the following common characteristics as below:

The developing countries may have these social challenges , they need to solve , such as :

(1) On social medical aspect

Closed economy/State Controlled economy or practice of socialism (which is in practice -one man/one party dictatorship). Low levels of literacy and esp. female literacy (less than 75% female literacy). Low health and HDI indicators (corresponding to the literacy levels). Low per capita income. High incidence of corruption, nepotism and kleptocracy.

The following is the path chosen by most of the former "low income/under developed/poor nations" to become developed (Germany & Japan post WW2, South Korea, Taiwan, Brazil, South Africa and China - some are still in process)- Economically liberal but politically/socially conservative regimes. Immense government spending (Keynesian economics) on - Infrastructure (Roads, Schools, Bridges, Ports, Airports, Power Plants, Hospitals and primary health centers etc).

(2) On international trade social aspect
Opening up the economy to international trade and foreign investments. Export oriented manufacturing practices, wherein the bulk of the population which was in the primary sector (agriculture, animal husbandry and mining etc) shifts to the secondary sector (manufacturing) and experiences corresponding increase in wages/income.
Application of procedures and rule of law on a gradual basis from the earlier arbitrariness which reigned supreme. The first step, in my view, is to make sure to have an honest and capable government that are committed to the development of the country and to the welfare of all people in the country. It is, in fact, the most difficult step to start with. Once we have a good and capable government, it is not so difficult to figure out or implement all steps necessary to make the country developed and prosper. On the other hand, having a corrupt, incapable, in other words, not only dishonest, but also stupid and foolish government means losing everything, no matter how abundance resource your country has, or how much foreign assistance and aids your country receives.
However, some economists believe that they are not "developing", but MAINTAINED IN PERMANENT

UNDERDEVELOPMENT on purpose. Market, same as everything, functions in 3D, the 3rd is the income strata. The “progress” is not for all the strata. Every upper stratum solves its own problems at expenses of pushing the next inferior one downwards (vertically) or over the edge (horizontally). Spend a few minutes on a search engine and you realize that the term “first world” is meaningless when referring to economic development. For example, Ireland, Switzerland and Sweden are examples of third world countries. A first world nation is one that allied with NATO as opposed to the Soviet Union during the Cold War.

(3) On solving social poverty aspect

Poverty is the default state of man. Knowledge is what allows us to go beyond our physical and cognitive limitations. With knowledge you can create technology that makes our lives better. At a base level, developing nations need a smaller percentage of their populations working in sustenance farming. This could be achieved by increases in farming productivity which would allow other people to specialize in making other goods and providing other services. Essentially creating more wealth.

Uaually, developing countries lack enough farming technology, they can’t specialize in something other than sustenance farming if 80% of your population farms with oxen instead of machines. This is where knowledge comes in play. Many developing nations have rich natural resources and commodities they just don’t have the knowledge necessary to turn it into something useful.

To summarize in one word what is necessary for a developing nation to become a developed one it is knowledge. Any one developing countries need to answer these questions, before they decide how to solve these social challenges in their development process as below:

What developing country will become the next developed nation? Why do they are developing countries ? How can they develop to be developed countries ? How long will it take for every country in the world to become developed? What is the way to develop a country? Which countries are likely to be developed countries soon?
For example, Brazilians is one developing country, because this country has high crime rate and poor rate is high and inflation is high. These are its social problems. As soon as hyperinflation and out-of-control crime was solved, Brazilians brought their money back to Brazil. The starting point for Brazilians is patriotism and nostalgia. Even with all the problems of corruption, taxes, bureaucracy and poor infrastructure if given a chance to make real money within the country a Brazilian will leave better opportunities in the US. So, Brazilians need to solve these social problems if this country hope to become one developed country in success. The easiest way to develop is: when each and every person decides to learn as much as possible, and decides to behave like civilized persons, who have total respect for all other persons' physical and patrimonial integrity. It's that easy and simple. But, often, the easiest things in life are the most difficult to learn.

- What a developing country should do to be a developed one?

The countries that developed the fastest often had the longest paths. If you compensate for that fact, then it becomes obvious that economic freedom is both necessary and sufficient. In particular, countries should avoid: socialism, i.e. collectivization of the means of production expropriation, i.e. robbing foreign investors of their properties autarchy, i.e. cutting all international trade. The less countries engage in these, the faster they develop.

● How can a developing country become a developed country?

Well, you could study economic history and learn how the present developed countries attained their present positions. There are also several examples in real time: look at how China and India are moving their countries from third world countries to developed economies. Two other interesting examples: Several African countries are using primarily cell phone techologies for communication and bypassing the infrastructure requirements for hardline technology. Ireland is well know to have been deforested when it's forests were harvested for the coal and fuel requirements of industrializing.

● Developed Countries need to help Developing Countries to increase their competitive effort in societies

IMPROVEMENTS IN HEALTH, EDUCATION AND TRADE ARE ESSENTIAL FOR THE DEVELOPMENT OF POORER NATIONS. HOWEVER,THE GOVERNMENTS OF RICHER NATIONS SHOULD TAKE MORE RESPONSIBILITY FOR HELPING THE POORER NATIONS IN SUCH AREAS.

Eliminate political tension by encouraging participation of all in the political, constitutional and economic processes. I recommend developed countries, such as US, UK can help developing countries to develop in sucess in these several aspects:

-Invest in infrastructure, education and health care.

-Encourage rural agriculture by providing agricultural inputs

and raising earned incomes.

-Raise levels of literacy

-Encourage the modern sectors of banking, manufacturing, retail, and extractive industries,

-Provide adequate sanitation and clean water

-Open the countries to direct foreign investments

-Remove trade barriers to exports and imports.

-Reduce dependency on single sectors that is diversification .

Can bring global benefit when all
countries are developed countries

1. How Globalization Affects Developed Countries

There are three perspective of globalization. Which are as : The Hyper globalist perspective: This says that economies are becoming Denationalized due to this government will lose it influence over the trade within its border. It will have both good and bad effects. The Skeptical perspective: it is kind based on myth that globalization will not help the under develop country as they do not perform a greater role in flow of trade and services in the global economy.

I assume that future one day, all countries can become developed countries. The globalization development effect will be caused by our global successful development. Does it means that globalization can only bring benefits ? I shall explain that when all countries can developed successfully. Globalization ought not only bring benefits to our global societies as below:

Globalization brings people and businesses together through the international exchange of money, ideas, and culture. However, some critics say it adversely affects developed countries. Opinions exist on both sides of the globalization debate. Proponents claim lower opportunity costs, producing positive growth, and reduced market volatility. At the same time, opponents decry the reduction of domestic job growth, cost of mismanagement to countries and the world, and the stagnation of wages.

Conflicting Globalization Views

U.S. President Donald Trump, for example, has been very vocal on his views of globalization and has taken a protectionist stance when it comes to free trade under agreements like the North American Free Trade Agreement (NAFTA), calling for higher taxes on imports and fewer multinational trade agreements. He has also increased tariffs on foreign goods to discourage their importation and use. No matter how much economists are quick to extol the universal benefits of globalization, some politicians and other economist demonize globalization as a force that takes away domestic jobs. These conflicting viewpoints have created a maelstrom of opinions and policies across developed countries that range from extreme protectionism through trade barriers, like President Trump's example, to complete openness.

From an economic standpoint, globalization is typically defined as the increase in the global trade of goods, services, capital, and technology. This growth in trade has been especially acute between developed countries like the United States and emerging markets, such as China. There are many factors behind the increase in global trade. European devastation after World War I and II helped to jumpstart America and an industrial superpower and exporter. Lower transportation costs have reduced the costs of trade, technologies have eliminated some barriers altogether, and liberal economic policies have helped lower political barriers to trade. While cost reductions have helped accelerate trade, the largest driver behind global trade is supply-demand economics and the desire to increase consumption on the part of both importers and exporters.

Benefits of globalization

The core benefit of globalization is the comparative advantage—that is, the ability of one country to produce goods or services at a lower opportunity cost than other countries. While the idea seems simple on the surface, it quickly becomes counterintuitive when examined more deeply. The theory suggests that two countries capable of producing two commodities at different costs can benefit the most by exporting the good where the comparative advantage exists. For example, a developing country may have a comparative advantage in producing cement, and the United States may have a comparative advantage in producing semiconductors. While the U.S. may be able to produce cement more efficiently than the developing country, the U.S. would still be better off focusing on semiconductors because of its comparative advantage. This is why globalization is powerful as a driver of global consumption between countries of all capabilities.

One of the major potential benefits of globalization is to provide opportunities for reducing macroeconomic volatility on output and consumption via diversification of risk. The overall evidence of the globalization effect on macroeconomic volatility of output indicates that although direct effects are ambiguous in theoretical models, financial integration helps in a nation's production base diversification, and leads to an increase in specialization of production. However, the specialization of production, based on the concept of comparative advantage, can also lead to higher volatility in specific industries within an economy and society of a nation. As time passes, successful companies, independent of size, will be the ones that are part of the global economy.

Empirical evidence suggests that a positive growth effect takes place in countries that are sufficiently rich when it comes to globalization. For investors and economies, globalization also provides the opportunity to reduce the volatility of output and consumption, since products and services can be imported or exported with greater ease. Fewer "bubbles" arise from a mismatch in supply and demand if the production of goods and services is more elastic. But, when all countries can develop to become developed countries, globalization developed countries which may also bring these disadvantages as below:

Drawbacks of globalization

Globalization is often criticized for taking away jobs from domestic companies and workers. After all, the U.S. cement industry will go out of business if imports from a developing country drive down prices, even if consumption increases. Small U.S. cement companies would find it difficult to compete and likely shut down, leaving workers unemployed, while the larger U.S. cement industry would likely experience a significant protracted decline.

A second criticism is the high cost of a comparative or absolute advantage to a country's own well-being if mismanaged. For example, China has become a leading worldwide emitter of carbon dioxide thanks to its comparative advantage in manufacturing a wide range of products. Other countries may have a comparative advantage in mining certain natural resources—such as crude oil—and mishandle the revenue generated from those activities.

A final disadvantage of globalization is the increase in wages for workers, which can hurt corporate profitability. For example, if a rich country has a high comparative advantage in developing software, they may drive up the price of software engineers around the world, which makes it difficult for foreign companies to compete in the market.

The phenomenon of globalization began in a primitive form when humans first settled into different areas of the world; however, it has shown a rather steady and rapid progress in recent times and has become an international dynamic which, due to technological advancements, has increased in speed and scale, so that countries in all five continents have been affected and engaged.

What Is Globalization? Why and how globalization may achieve when global countries can develop to become developed countries ?

Globalization is defined as a process that, based on international strategies, aims to expand business operations on a worldwide level, and was precipitated by the facilitation of global communications due to technological advancements, and socioeconomic, political and environmental developments.

The goal of globalization is to provide organizations a superior competitive position with lower operating costs, to gain greater numbers of products, services, and consumers. This approach to competition is gained via diversification of resources, the creation and development of new investment opportunities by opening up additional markets and accessing new raw materials and resources. Diversification of resources is a business strategy that increases the variety of business products and services within various organizations. Diversification strengthens institutions by lowering organizational risk factors, spreading interests in different areas, taking advantage of market opportunities, and acquiring companies both horizontal and vertical in nature.

Industrialized or developed nations are specific countries with a high level of economic development and meet certain socioeconomic criteria based on economic theory, such as gross domestic product (GDP), industrialization and human development index (HDI) as defined by the International Monetary Fund (IMF), the United Nations (UN) and the World Trade Organization (WTO). Using these definitions, some industrialized countries are: United Kingdom, Belgium, Denmark, Finland, France, Germany, Japan, Luxembourg, Norway, Sweden, Switzerland, and the United States.

Components of Globalization

The components of globalization include GDP, industrialization and the Human Development Index (HDI). The GDP is the market value of all finished goods and services produced within a country's borders in a year and serves as a measure of a country's overall economic output. Industrialization is a process which, driven by technological innovation, effectuates social change and economic development by transforming a country into a modernized industrial, or developed nation. The Human Development Index comprises three components: a country's population's life expectancy, knowledge and education measured by the adult literacy, and income.

The degree to which an organization is globalized and diversified has bearing on the strategies that it uses to pursue greater development and investment opportunities. When all countries can become developed countries. They may bring the Economic Impact on Developed Nations as below: Globalization compels businesses to adapt to different strategies based on new ideological trends that try to balance the rights and interests of both the individual and the community as a whole. This change enables businesses to compete worldwide and also signifies a dramatic change for business leaders, labor and management by legitimately accepting the participation of workers and government in developing and implementing company policies and strategies. Risk reduction via diversification can be accomplished through company involvement with international financial institutions and partnering with both local and multinational businesses.

Globalization brings reorganization at the international, national and sub-national levels. Specifically, it brings the reorganization of production, international trade and the integration of financial markets. This affects capitalist economic and social relations, via multilateralism and microeconomic phenomena, such as business competitiveness, at the global level. The transformation of production systems affects the class structure, the labor process, the application of technology and the structure and organization of capital. Globalization is now seen as marginalizing the less educated and low-skilled workers. Business expansion will no longer automatically imply increased employment. Additionally, it can cause a high remuneration of capital, due to its higher mobility compared to labor.

The phenomenon seems to be driven by three major forces: the globalization of all product and financial markets, technology, and deregulation. Globalization of product and financial markets refers to an increased economic integration in specialization and economies of scale, which will result in greater trade in financial services through both capital flows and cross-border entry activity. The technology factor, specifically telecommunication and information availability, has facilitated remote delivery and provided new access and distribution channels, while revamping industrial structures for financial services by allowing entry of non-bank entities, such as telecoms and utilities.

When all countries can become developed countries. In a global economic view, power is the ability of a company to command both tangible and intangible assets that create customer loyalty, regardless of location. Independent of size or geographic location, a company can meet global standards and tap into global networks, thrive and act as a world-class thinker, maker, and trader, by using its greatest assets: its concepts, competence, and connections. When all developing countries become developed countries, they may bring these beneficial effects as below:

Some economists have a positive outlook regarding the net effects of globalization on economic growth. These effects have been analyzed over the years by several studies attempting to measure the impact of globalization on various nations' economies using variables such as trade, capital flows, and their openness, GDP per capita, foreign direct investment (FDI) and more. These studies examined the effects of several components of globalization on growth using time-series cross-sectional data on trade, FDI and portfolio investment. Although they provide an analysis of individual components of globalization on economic growth, some of the results are inconclusive or even contradictory. However, overall, the findings of those studies seem to be supportive of the economists' positive position, instead of the one held by the public and non-economist view.

Trade among nations via the use of comparative advantage promotes growth, which is attributed to a strong correlation between the openness to trade flows and the effect on economic growth and economic performance. Additionally, there is a strong positive relation between capital flows and their impact on economic growth. Foreign Direct Investment's impact on economic growth has had a positive growth effect in wealthy countries and an increase in trade and FDI, resulting in higher growth rates.8 Empirical research examining the effects of several components of globalization on growth, using time series and cross-sectional data on trade, FDI and portfolio investment, found that a country tends to have a lower degree of globalization if it generates higher revenues from trade taxes. Further evidence indicates that there is a positive growth-effect in countries that are sufficiently rich, as are most of the developed nations.

The World Bank reports that integration with global capital markets can lead to disastrous effects, without sound domestic financial systems. One of the potential benefits of globalization is to provide opportunities for reducing macroeconomic volatility on output and consumption via diversification of risk.

However, when all countries can become developed countries, they may also bring these harmful effects as below:

Non-economists and the wide public expect the costs associated with globalization to outweigh the benefits, especially in the short-run. Less wealthy countries from those among the industrialized nations may not have the same highly-accentuated beneficial effect from globalization as more wealthy countries, measured by GDP per capita, etc. Although free trade increases opportunities for international trade, it also increases the risk of failure for smaller companies that cannot compete globally. Additionally, free trade may drive up production and labor costs, including higher wages for a more skilled workforce, which again can lead to outsourcing jobs from countries with higher wages. Moreover, domestic industries in some countries may be endangered due to comparative or absolute advantage of other countries in specific industries. Another possible danger and harmful effect is the overuse and abuse of natural resources to meet new higher demands in the production of goods.

In overall, when all countries can develop to become developed countries, they may bring these general benefits to influence our society to bring positive changes. They may include: Globalization activity doesn't only reduce trade boundary but it lot more effects like one country come closer to the economy of other country, it help in mixture of culture, it helps in transfer information and technology, increase group of buyer and seller of products and services etc. this are only few advantages of globalizations. Due to globalization trade is getting more interdependent and to protect interest of every nation W.T.O keep a close look over the trade of every nation. Due globalization many environmental threats are evolved every country is moving toward industrialization which increase global warming and it is needed to be checked. Social problem are also occurred like exploitation of labour, increase in child labour in developing nations, lack of powerful labour union etc this social problem are needed to taken care of and proper law should be made to avoid such kind of problems. As every things as has some advantages, it also has some disadvantages also.

Advantages:

- New market for product.
- Helps in growth of economy.
- Increase in infrastructure.
- Free flow of technology and information.
- Reduction in poverty.
- Increases in employments.

- International body governs trade through its law, so interest of every country should be protected.

Disadvantages are as follows:

- It brings competitions because of which small scale industries suffer in under develop countries.
- Globalization lead to growth in infrastructure but on other hand it bring harm to environment due to industrialization, reduction in forest areas.
- Due to globalization environment, labour, resource of under develop countries are exploited by develop countries.
- Poor trade union.
- Lack of control over country economy by its governments.

Effect of globalization on developing countries or third world countries

The thinking of first world, second world and third world countries are given by U.S.A which place itself as the first world nation, European countries as second world nations and as far as third world country are concerned under develop and developing countries come under this categories. The third world countries are further classified as under developed countries and developing countries. In under developed, countries like Afghanistan, Nepal, Bangladesh, Nigeria, Bhutan, Pakistan etc comes this are the growing nations but as far as development of economy is concerned they are far behind. In developing countries, countries like China, India, South Africa, Brazil etc are included because this are among fastest growing nation after globalization has taken place. But under develop countries are not much benefited because of this globalization process. Rather than getting benefit they are exploited. In a sense, due to cheap labour these countries manpower is exploited and it natural resource is been taken away as we can take the example of china, china is investing a lot in African nation and on exchange of this it is utilizing its natural resources.

What influences to the countries like china and India has grown tremendously after globalization.

Before globalizations export of china was not very high but now it is one the global leader in exports and as far as India is concerned before India was accounted only for 0.6 % of world export and now it is accounted for 1 % of world exports. Brazil has also show huge growth its per capita income has also increased. Countries like Bhutan, Malaysia, Indonesia etc has tremendous growth in GDP in past five years. Outsourcing has increased in these nations. Now India earns 51% of GDP from service sectors and its service sector is growing tremendously because of it excellence in IT sectors and this boosted up after globalizations. Now china earns major part of it GDP from export which increased after globalization. As far as Latin America is concerned Brazil has show tremendous growth in export, technology and manufacturing sectors. And now it is among top five of developing nations.

Effect of globalization on developed countries when all developing countries can become developed countries

Due to globalization the develop countries are moving towards underdeveloped countries like India, China, Indonesia etc for outsourcing their job to these countries because of cheap labour. Nowadays develop nation are coming to under develop nation for setting up manufacturing plants in these nation because of its availability of cheap and skilled labours. Due to globalization develop countries are facing intense competition from underdeveloped countries, competition in sense employment, exports, technology etc. Due to globalization developed countries are also exploit resources like natural resource, manpower, and environment etc. of underdeveloped nations. Also, due to globalization the dominance of developed nation is also reducing. The people of developed nation are facing intense competition for job from people growing nation like china, India, Thailand etc. now for FDI in developed nation are reducing due increase in the FDI in developing countries like china, Brazil, India etc. Thus, when all developing countries can develop to become developed countries in future one day. Globalization developed countries got new market for their products and services, and new place for their business expansions.

Development of "Regional economic" will truly help India to build viable economic future for its citizens.

Due to globalization various effect and development has take place which help india to build viable economic future for its citizens. Due Globalization to this the infrastructure of India has developed a lot because of which transportation, sanitary, hygiene, sports complex and stadium has developed a lot and still developing which will give better environment for future generation. Nowadays, foreign education institutes are coming to india which has increased the level of education. Export of india is increasing with each quarter which help to reduce the fiscal deficit and increase the GDP of the nation.

Nowadays more and more manufacturing industries are established because of which more employment is created and hence improving per capita income of the nation. Due globalization India is more concerned about the global warming and planning its growth in such a way that it could reduce it contribution in global. And it will be helpful for future citizens.

Regional economies help to reduce domination of developed economies on the developing economies.

Developments in regional economy will strength the self reliability of the nation which will help to reduction in the dependence on other nation. Development of regional economy will lead to increase in GDP, Standard of living, Per capita income of the nation. If India wants to emerge as supper power it has to develop it regional because it is the stepping stone toward it.

In conclusion, when all countries can develop to achieve developed countries. They will create development of regional economy to our global societies. Then, they may bring these benefits in possible. They may include: Development of regional economy will lead to reduce in inequalities of distribution of wealth, development of regional economy will lead to increase in metropolitan culture, development of regional economy will lead increase the contributions of every state in Indian GDP, development of regional economy will lead to reduction of poverty, unemployment and illiteracy.

2. Economic growth advantages and disadvantages

When all developing countries can develop to be developed countries, then it may also bring global economic growth. However, I believe that when global societies can have sudden economic growth in short time, due to all or many developing countries can develop to be developed countries in success. They may bring advantages and disadvantages both aspects as below:

Economic development can be describe as the development of economic wealth of countries or regions for the well-being of their inhabitants such as the improvement and innovation on the political, economic, and social of its people. Economic development and growth are totally different in terms which are used in economics. Economic development refers to economic growth which accompanied by changes in economic structure and output distribution. So, economic growth may be necessary but not sufficient to attain economic development. Thus, peoples always said that economic development is the problems of underdeveloped countries and economic growth to those of developed countries. Underdeveloped countries always face some problems such as low income, weakness of human resource and also the economic vulnerability. These problems also made the countries hard to attain the development of economic. However, for those developed countries, they do not face the same problems as what underdeveloped countries do, therefore, they are more easily to attain the economic development and treat it as an economic growth.

In addition, in the term of economic development is much more comprehensive because it implies progressive changes in the socio-economic structure of a country. Nowadays, the evolution of new technology is directly related to economic development. Without high technology in a country, it is hard to bring an economic development toward its people. Viewed in this way economic development involves a steady decline in agricultural shares in GNP and continuous increase in shares of industries, trade banking construction and services. However, economic growth just only refers to the rise in total output in a country; development implies change in technological and institutional organization of production as well as in distributive pattern of income.

Hence, if compared to the goal of development, economic growth is much easy to realize. Between, we just need a larger mobilization of resources and raising their productivity by enhance it to be more efficiency and effective, then the output level can be raised and economic growth will occur. However, the development process is far more extensive than the economic growth. Not only a rise in output, it also involved changes in composition of output, and shift in the allocation of productive resources, and reduction or elimination of poverty, inequalities and unemployment. However, economic development is impossible without having an economic growth but economic growth is possible without an economic development. Growth is just increase in GNP but it does not have any other parameters to it; unlike development which can be conceived as Multi-Dimensional process.

Are economic growth and development worthwhile? Economic growth and development have their advantages and also disadvantages. Although economic growth widens the range of human choices, but this may not necessarily bring happiness toward people. Happiness is dependent on the relationship between wants and resources. People may become more satisfied, not only by having more wants met, but perhaps also by renouncing certain material goods. Wealth may make people less happy if it increases wants more than resources. Furthermore, acquisitive and achievement-oriented societies may be more likely to give rise to individual frustration.

Advantages

Economic growth will decreases famine, starvation, infant mortality, and death; gives us greater leisure; can enhance art, music, and philosophy; and gives us the resources to be humanitarian. Economic growth will especially benefit to societies in which political desire exceed the resources, because it may prevent what might otherwise prove to be social tension that people can't take it. However, without economic growth, the desires of one group can be met when others expense on it. Lastly, economic growth can help newly independent countries in mobilizing resources to increase the power of a nation.

Disadvantages

Growth has its value. First, the disadvantage might be the acquisitiveness, materialism, and dissatisfaction with one's present state associated with a society's economic struggles. Second, liquidity, objective, and self-associated with economic growth may undermine the reliance on extended family system, in fact, the focus of the prevailing social structure. Third, economic growth, which depends on the rational and technological innovation and changes in scientific methods, often is the threat in religious and social authority. Fourth, economic growth often require more specialized work, which may be caused by more objective, accompanied more drab and monotonous tasks, more discipline, and a pair of process loss.

In addition, economic growth which follow by large organizational units are more likely to lead to bureaucratization, objective, communication problems, and the use of force were consistent. Economic growth and development of large enterprises with a manufacturer's products and services while demand increased, and urban growth, this may be is accompanied byrootlessness, environmental blight disease, and unhealthy living conditions, even in the narrow social values change and may ultimately lead to a new dynamic equilibrium that is better than the old static equilibrium, the transition could have some very painful issues. In addition, the political transformation, as rapid economic growth, may lead to greater concentration, stress, social disruption, even authoritarian. Therefore, even if the population seriously committed to economic growth, its implementation is not likely at all costs pursued. All societies must take into account that the conflicts with the maximization of economic growth and other objectives. Because it was want sits in high level positions, a developing country own citizens can promote the local production control to reduce the growth in the short term.

The question now is what will be weighed to achieve an orderly, stable society, and maintain traditional values and culture, and promoting political autonomy? Economic growth is the increase a country's per capita output. Economic development, economic growth has resulted in the poorest strata of the population or level of education, changes to improve the output distribution of economic welfare and economic changes in different structures.

Economic growth and development of Asia when all or many developing countries can develop to be developed countries

Nowadays, economic development in Asia shows high impact of economic development of this respective continent. Economy of Asia has taken an important part in the view of the world's economy. These continents have adopted one of the following economic systems such as capitalism, socialism, communism, and fascism. As we know, Asia is the largest continent in terms of area surface and also the population. Beside it, it is also the region with the highest growth rate. Below are Asian countries that contribute their economic development to our society.

Of all the Asian Countries, the only Asian country included

among the industrialized countries is Japan. According to the International Monetary Fund, the country per capita was GDP 32,608 U.S. dollars or in 2009, the 23rd highest on record. Moreover, according to certain criteria, the term means that developed countries is the countries that having a high level of development. What standards and which countries are classified as being developed, is a controversial issue which surrounded by a fierce debate. Thus, economic criteria tend to dominate discussions. Countries which having per capita income and high per capita gross domestic product (GDP) will be described as developed countries. Another criterion is the industrialization; countries in the tertiary and quaternary sector-of industry leading will be described as development. Another recent measure, the human development index, which combines economic measures, and other measures of national income, life expectancy and education indicators, have become prominent. This criterion will define the development country as those very high (HDI) rating. However, many exceptions exist when the decision to "developed country" status is used to measure the subject. Countries do not fit this definition are classified as developing countries.

However, Taiwan, Hong Kong and Singapore are regarded as newly industrialized countries. The category of newly industrialized country (NIC) is a socioeconomic classification which applied to various countries in the world by political scientists and economists. NIC is the nation's economy has not yet reached first world status, but in the macro sense, the development of the countries is normally faster than counterpart. Another feature of newly industrialized countries is that undergoing in rapid economic growth (usually export-oriented). However, the starting or ongoing industrialization is an important indicator of NIC. In many newly industrialized countries, may also be experiencing social unrest by major primary rural, or agricultural, populations migrate to the cities, where the thousand of laborers can be draw by growth of manufacturing concerns and factories. In the social development process, it usually shares some characteristic such as increased social freedoms and civil rights, strong political leadership, which switch from an agricultural to an industrial economy, the other common features, especially in the manufacturing sector, an increasingly open market economy with free trade and other heavy capital investment from countries around the world. In addition, the political leadership in their area of influence and lastly is they have lowered poverty rates.

I shall indicate China, Philippines, India, North Korea these developing country when they can become developed country , what it can bring global social change influence example. Moreover, as we know, the history and culture of China is their secret to improve their economy, even if it ruled and control by their state. Prior to 1979, China maintained a centrally planned or command economy. The economy of China with the large proportion is directed by the state which established production goals, controlled prices, distribution, and most of the economic control of resources. During the 1950s, all of China's individual household farms were collectivized into large communes. To support rapid industrialization, the central government starts to take large-scale physical and human capital investment during 1960-1970s. As a result, by 1978, nearly three quarters of industrial production generated by the central control of state-owned enterprises according to centrally planned output targets. Private enterprises and foreign invested enterprises are almost non-existent.

A central objective of Chinese government was to make China's economy relatively self-sufficient. Foreign trade was generally limited to those commodity which unable to obtain or receive the goods in China. The Government's policy to keep the Chinese economy relatively stagnant and inefficient, mainly because of where the profits of some enterprises and farmers to stimulate competition, in fact, does not exist, price and production controls caused widespread economic distortions. China's standard of living is much lower than those of many other.

In addition, India is contributing in business process outsourcing improvement for the information technology which has a significant impact for the economic development in South Asia. The Philippines is improving, because they help to remittances from abroad, they send money to their loved ones from overseas Filipino workers to improve their country. North Korea shows hammer and sling as a symbol for their communistic views of their economic system in Far East Asia. While South Korea shows modern technology that is influence from Western countries which results an improvement of technology in their designated countries. Indonesia is a Muslim country, the whole of Asia's largest population by the Dutch colony. It is based on their banking and finance in the Islamic way of life. This is also the case in Malaysia was a British colony. After analyze the information of some Asian Countries, I discovered that they are facing several problems in economic development. First, they have low standard of living, low level of production, there is a rapid population growth, they having a high rate of unemployment, lastly, there are over dependence on agricultural production and exportation of raw materials and also the international trade.

Economic growth and development of Malaysia According to the recent The Star's newspaper, Malaysia economic development is one of fastest and steady in global economic scenario. Malaysia GDP per capita has been estimated to be $15,700 in fiscal year 2008. This is a clear indication of tremendous economic development in Malaysia. Malaysia economy is a middle income country that has developed since 1970's. It was previously a mere raw materials producing economy, which has evolved now as a developing multi-sector economy. This growth bears testimony to impressive economic development at Malaysia. Prime Minister Abdullah, after coming to power in 2003, has tried to develop economy of this south Asian country by introducing value added production. He took a number of measures to introduce hi-tech technologies and encouraged investments in high technology industries, medical technology and pharmaceuticals. Efforts have been made by government of Malaysia to stop its dependence on export products. However, exports of electronics goods have always been a major factor in Malaysia economy. There has been huge profit accrued from export of oil and gas and it has been a major factor for Malaysia economic development. There have been huge profits from high energy prices, although there was high cost of gasoline and diesel fuel. This, however, made Kuala Lumpur minimize financial assistance of government. It has been found that currency value of Malaysia has hiked 6 percent per year when pitted against dollar in fiscal years 2006 to 2008.

Model of economy development: The production function how can be influenced to change when many or all developing countries can become developed countries

In macroeconomics, the production function is a function which specifies combination of all input from the output. In the macro-economy, production functions are functions that determine the output of a company which entered all combinations of input. A meta-production function comparing the practices of companies that has to change input to output to determine the function of the most efficient production practices of the entity that is, whether the most efficient production practices that qualify or production practices that are actually the most efficient. In these cases, the maximum output production process technology is defined as mathematical function of one or more entered. In other words, given a collection of all technical combination allows the output and input, just include a combination of maximum output for a given set of inputs to the production or function. Production function can be defined as specification of minimum input requirements needed to produce a total output that was, by given current technology. It is usually assumed that the production of unique functions can be built for every production technology.

Assuming when many or all developing countries can develop to become developed countries in future one day, they may bring these influences to our social technologic production function changes as below:

The maximum output possible from the set of technology inputs of all, the economic use in the production function analysis is the abstract essence of the technical and managerial problems associated with a specific production process. Engineering and managerial problems of technical competence is assumed to be broken, so the analysis can focus on the problem of efficiency allocate. States are assumed to make choices about how much each input of allocate factors put to use and how much output to produce, remember the cost (purchase price) of each factor, the sale price of output, and the factors represent technology to determine its production function. Frame results in one or more constant input can be used, for example, capital can be assumed to be fixed (constant) in the short term, and labor and possibly other variables such as input raw material, while in the long run, the quantity of capital and the factors that can be made by the company are variable. In the long term, companies may even have the choice of technology, represented by the various functions of production as possible.

Input to output relationship is non-financial, that the production function relating physical inputs to physical outputs, and prices and the cost is reflected in the function. But the production function is not a complete model of the production process: intentionally abstract from the inherent aspects of physical production process that some would consider extremely important, including error, entropy or waste. In addition, the production functions do not typically model business processes, well, ignoring the role of management. (For primer on the basic elements of the production of Microeconomics theory, see production theory policies).

The main purpose of the production function is to address allocate efficiency in the use of input factors in production and distribution of factory income such factors. Based on certain assumptions, the production function can be used to reduce a marginalized product for each factor, which implies an ideal division of the revenue generated from the output to the income from their every input factor of production.

How global developed economy influences household expenditure decision?

In the saving function, there is a mathematical relation between saving and income by the household sector. Thus, the saving function can be stated as an equation such as a simple linear equation or a diagram indicated as the saving line. This function captures the relationship between savings and income, one of the other sides the relationship between consumer incomes, constitutes a cornerstone of Keynesian economics. The two key function to save the parameters are intercept, which indicates that self-saving, side slope, which is the marginal propensity to save, show that the induced savings. The injection- leakage model used in Keynesian economics is based on the saving function.
Saving function on Keynesian economics is the starting point for determination of equilibrium output injection, leakage model. It captures the household sector in which the relationship between savings and income. As the income for either consumption or savings to use, saving feature is the complementary consumption function. Reflects the fundamental psychological law put forward by John Maynard Keynes, consumer spending (and saving by the household sector) depends on the income and just some of the revenue is used for consumption and saving the rest. This function is presented either as a mathematical formula, usually as a simple linear equation, graph or savings line. In either form, income is a measure of disposable income, national income and GDP. However, the saving function makes it easy to divide saving into two basic types such as the autonomous saving and Induced saving. Autonomous saving is the intercept term. Induced saving is the slope. Lastly, the slope of marginal propensity to save (MPS) also considered as saving function

How global developed economy influences the labor supply function changes ?

In mainstream economic theory, labor supply is the total number of hours number of a workers want to work in a given real wage rate. From the diagram above, we can see the positive relationship between the wages rate and also the quantity of labor. When the wage rate is low, the quantity of the labor also is low. However, when there is a rose in wage rate will also increase the quantity of labor. Realistically, the labor supply is the role of various factors within an economy. For example, as a heavy increased of population will make downward pressure on wages which may lead to high unemployment.

How global developed economy influences wage rate versus labor leisure changes?

Labor supply curves are derived from the 'labor-leisure' trade-off. More hours worked earn higher incomes but necessitate a cut in the amount of leisure that workers enjoy. Therefore, there are two aspects, to provide the necessary amount of labor is due to changes in real wage rates. For example, the real wage rate raises the opportunity cost of leisure increases as the diagram shows above. This tends to cause workers to supply more labor (the "substitution effect"). However, as the real wage rate rises, workers earn a higher income for a given number of hours. If leisure is a normal good – the demand for it increases as income increases – this increase in income will tend to cause workers to supply less labor (the "income effect"). If the "substitution effect" is stronger than the "income effect" then the labor supply curve will be upward sloping and vice versa.

However, from the view of Marxist, a labor supply is a core requirement in a capitalist society. In order to avoid Labor shortage and ensure a labor supply, a large portion of the population must not possess sources of self-provisioning, which would allow them to be independent, and they must instead be compelled, in order to survive, to sell their labor for a subsistence wage.

Economic development theories: Harrod-Domar theory When all or many countries can develop to be developed countries, how they can influence global technological growth rate changes. The Harrod-Domar theory delineates a functional economic relationship in which the growth rate of gross domestic product (g) depends directly on the national saving ratio (s) and inversely on the national capital/output ratio (k) so that it is written a $g = s / k$. The equation takes its name from a synthesis of analyses of growth process by two economists (Sir Roy Harrod of Britain and E.V. Domar of the USA). The Harrod-Domar model in the early postwar times was commonly used by developing countries in economic planning. With a target growth rate, the required saving rate is known. If the country is not capable of generating that level of saving, a justification or an excuse for borrowing from international agencies can be established. An example in the Asian context is to ascertain the relationship between high growth rates and high saving rates in the cases of Japan and China. It is more difficult to introduce the third building block of a growth model, the labor and population element. In the long run, growth rate is constrained by population growth and also by the rate of technological change.

● Climate change will impact developed countries to continue develop

Will developed countries become
developing countries

- Why does illness can cause global economic recession to developed countries

Firstly, I shall explain why unpredicted illness factor can cause developed countries' economic recession. Although developed countries have advantages and let people to believe that their any medical, economic, education, business etc. different industries aspects are developed in mature. Their these any industries aspects are better or are improved better to compare the developing countries. But, in fact, whether it is possible that their any industries aspects will become worse to compare developing countries when they do not continue to improve any one of their industries aspects. I shall indiate whether what factors my cause developed countries to become developing countries in possible.

Many developing countries are facing problem very different from that of the developed countries. Countries such as Japan, Germany are facing depleting population whether on the other side countries like India, Indonesia are facing severe resource crunch due to population explosion. In such situation measuring the progress of the countries on the same scales decided by developed industrialized world is injustice to these countries. Developed world have achieved there parameters after journey of around 200-250 years post industrialization while many developing countries are in their 60s-70s after getting freedom from crutches of colonialism. In such cases developing countries should formulate their own parameters for growth and development and continue their progress. So, it seems that any developing countries will have possible to develop to be better any developed countries. Otherwise, any developed countries will have possible to bring worse development when they have many people loss jobs. For example, US economy will go down nowadays, due to the Chinese serious illness influences many US people die. Many US businessmen can not continue to manufacture or sell their products because many people can not go to offices or factories to work. They need to stay at homes to avoid the illness attacks when they need to contact the illness people in workplace, or they are walking on streets, or they are catching any public transport. So,although US is one developed country, but it can not still to avoid this China illness attack. It is possible due to US government neglects to consider this China illness is one kind of death sick to cause US has many people to die easily in this year 2020. If US government can prohibit to let Chinese travellers to enter its country when China has occurred this serious illness caused in 2019 last year. These Chiness illness people can not enter US to cause this kind of illness to attack any US people lung to cause they die. After it is possible that US can avoid to cause many US people to die. So, it does not consider whether the country is developed or not to avoid global economic recession, because it is illness factor to cause developed countries' economic recession, such as US, UK nowadays economic recession.

● Increasing social crime rate and government assistance may cause developed countries to become developing coutries

Secondly, I shall explain why increasing social crime rate or many young people do criminal behaviors in society, it can influence developed countries to develop worse or can not develop better in its society. Otherwise, when on developing countries have less crime rate or decreases its crime rate, it can develop better or improve its society to be better. For a developing country to catch up to a developed country, it must not only grow, but grow faster than the developed country. While It is possible for such accelerated growth to occur through rapid industrialization, but there are many country-specific factors that directly affect a developing country's ability to catch up to developed countries. They range from growth of productivity, labour force participation rate, standard of living, infrastructure, political environment etc.

For example, when the developing country can improve its education quality to let many young people learn any kinds of new knowledge to like do any kinds of jobs, even, driving , factory labor, waiters, etc. low educational level jobs in society. Then, it will reduce its crime rate when many young people feel need to work. They won't need government to assist their life. Consequently, it will have possible to develop its economy or improve its economy to be better. In education primarily is the most essential quality that helps to empower the people of the country to communicate and achieve a common objective and is thus an extremely important driver for the developing to developed country journey. This is a common observation in all the developing countries. The one area that is still a struggle is education. Also, lack of education leads to increased poverty and disparity of income which leads to the 2nd most hindrance in a countries journey to achieve a developed nation status. Maybe if the path chosen is that of streamlining lack of education, poverty, a more driven and focused effort with individuals who know and can fathom the importance of this change working towards achieving a developed nation status can be undertaken. A semi-industrial, pro-human development approach should be a path adopted to see a qualitative shift in reducing this gap. All through our education we have learnt 'India is a developing country' which brings to thought, will it ever be recognized as a 'developed country'? And what is the criteria to qualify as a developed nation? Are these criteria set by the developed nations to meet their convenience? If this is the case it would be more logical for developing nations to set their own criteria. It gets very difficult for developing nations to meet the criteria set by the giant economies, as even a single step gone wrong could ruin the effort of years. India can be seen as an example, where the step of demonetization and GST together led to a growth rate of 5.7%, weakest growth rate since the first quarter of 2014. These steps would probably have a positive effect in the long run and it is worth the wait. Another question to bring our attention to is, are the developed countries developed in the true sense? Considering the parameter of crime rate, USA has a very high crime rate. Another aspect could be unemployment, again US has a good percent of unemployed individuals every year. So, aren't the developed nations also falling short? It may be a good strategy for developing nations could be establishing a path which would help them use their resources aptly and generate output for their people.

In this race of matching with the developed nations we are leading nowhere, better we set a different goal all together. Every nation has a different potential given different kinds of resources they possess hence expecting the same output from all makes little sense. Hope the coming generation gets to learn, 'India is a developed country in the true sense'. Hence, high crime rate, such as US has high crime rate. Because it has many young people do not like to work, they depend on government assistance. Then, any kinds of low skill or low educational level job employers will feel difficult to find them to work. Then, their society will cause low skillful labour shortage challange. It is not due to US lacks enough low skill or low educational workers, it is due to they do not like to work, they feel wages are less , when their government can give any money or loss job allowance to support their lives in long time. It can enough these low educational level or low skillful level young people choose not work. Then, this US developed country will not have any young people to do any service job, e.g. driving public transport, waiter, security. When these kinds of job old people need to retire, these employers can not find any young people to replace them to do these service jobs. They can only choose to employ another old age people to replace the retired service staffs. Then, these kinds any one of service jobs can not raise their service level, their service performance will be worse or keep the same service level, it means that their performance can not perform better level to serve their clients in US society. It implies that developed country, such as US its general social service level will be worse or they can not be improved to satisfy their client needs. In this developed country's poor service environment, how to explain it can still keep its developed country's position , such as US.

However, it may bring the question -Will Developing Countries ever catch up with Developed Countries? will remain unanswered because you have rightly pointed out that leaders of developing countries have given up on the economy and they keep themselves busy with other matters. Political institutions has great impact on the development of a nation. Industrial revolution happened in England instead of any other country because England had the best political institution that time. We have been hearing that if the 20th century belonged to developed countries of North America and Europe then 21st century will be of developing countries such as India, China and Brazil. But development is the crucial word which draws boundary between two countries-developed or developing. According to the World Bank reducing poverty is the main purpose of the development. After the World War 2, many nations have had significant growth however only few have been able to catch up with developed countries in terms of per capita income. From 1940s till 1990s poor countries grew slowly, falling farther behind to rich ones in income. Only few countries such as South Korea and Singapore were able to gain rich status. Since 2000, developing nations such as India and China are economically growing and managing growth rates of above 10% per year. With such continuous growth rates, developing nations can converge with developed nations and that would mean higher standard of living and good economic and political power. But this growth is limited to few countries since many countries still have not opened their domestic market to international markets. These countries also have barriers in technology and availability and allocation of resources. So, it seems that developing countries still need more time to develop exceed to the developed countries because they, such as China, Korea, Taiwan , Singapore etc. have poor technology and shortage of allocation or resource to compare the developed countries, such as US, UK etc. even their crime rate may reduce or many young people may accept to do the low skillful or low education level service jobs in societies.

● Developed countries lack effort to manufacture cheap products to sell strengths

Hence, we need to look at every economy as a company and developing a unique selling proposition becomes relevant. The United States has a USP of being the most technologically advanced and productive country. China has managed to become an exporter of cheap goods, the United Kingdom till now was a financial hub- there are chances of that changing thanks to BREXIT with the rise of Dublin. When we look at developing economies, such as India, we do not see any USP in the making. What is India's USP? I cannot think of any. People talk about demographic dividend to India in terms of a large young population. Such a population, which is largely uneducated is a demographic curse. Merely being a large market for goods and services is a bad idea for a USP. Developing countries need to introspect sometimes to look at the systemic challenges that they face. Looking towards developed economies is not always the best alternative. Such as China can choose to buy cheap product, because its technologic developement is poor. It is its strength to manufacture cheap products to sell to overseas to earn foreign income and raise GDP on export aspect. So, China may have much development chance to grow up its economy when it can decide which kinds of cheap or easier manufacturing products to sell to overseas when these countries can not supply from themselves manufactures, they need to buy from China in long time.

While the share of many western economies remained very low. However, over the years the trend started to reverse and many western countries have now become very developed while third world countries like India, China etc. continue on their journey from being developing to developed. We are currently a 2 trillion dollar economy and the eighth largest economy in the world. By 2030, India is predicted to be the fifth largest economy in the world. On purchasing power basis, India is the second largest economy in the world only behind China. Despite so many bright spots, we are faced with the paradox of being an advanced economy and still being one of the poorest in the world.

Otherwise, many such countries who are highly rich in natural resources continue to be plundered by the developed economies. Many countries continue to be haunted by the choices they made in past and turnaround being highly unlikely. They are often not helped by the injustices meted out by the developed economies who continue to take decision in their own self-interest. I feel the time has come when all the developing economies need to unite and raise their voice collectively. They need to speak about the unfair treatment meted out to them. A step in this regard has been taken by countries like India and China in important forums like UN and WTO. These breakout countries can act like role models and help create a more equitable world.

Another country is India, developing country , it may choose to manufacture and sell cheap products to any overeas countries to earn high GDP trade income. Till about 1750s, India was one of the largest economies in the world, contributing close to 25% of the world GDP. It was called the 'Golden Bird' and its products were world famed. The country has had huge trade surpluses for centuries through export of spices, finished cloth ('light woven air', it was called), and diamonds; all exotic products to that time period. It also had a thriving shipbuilding industry. There were accounts of Roman Establishments worrying about their riches syphoning off to India, because of the love of their woman towards Indian Cloth. India, thus essentially provided what the world desired & craved for, taking very few in return. This is despite the fact that it had one of the largest populations of that time. Then how come Indians achieve that richness and advancement, which seems difficult now? It is because, India was a hotbed of skilled people, who created exotic products, which were taken to the world by merchants in Indian built ships, which in turn were financed adequately by an established network of local people. So, although, India is not one high technologic development country, but it can choose what kinds of general cheap products to manufacture or catch any natural resources, e.g. growing up fishing industry, diamond industry. It is any one developed countries can not own strengths to compete to India easily.

Modern India and the ilk, are that they should spend more on Education and encourage Individual/SMEs (Small and Medium scale Enterprises), through adequate financing. The educational infrastructure should go to every nook and corner of the country like the 'temple complexes' providing accessible and affordable education, in the form of 'community colleges' in the US & 'skill enhancement centres'. Governments should support with adequate funds to create world-class universities of yesterday like 'The Nalanda', to provide cross-functional education and focus on innovation. The population should be encouraged to innovate & produce products, the world desires, like the 'light muslin cloth' or the 'iPhone' of the modern day, which shall bring huge trade surpluses. Industrialization should be decentralized through support for SMEs rather than purely going for High scale Industries. The financial infrastructure should be expanded enough to provide the financial support to every citizen, through banking services. Thus, on the whole, history can provide us with a lot of lessons on how to go about things, provided we have the interest to see from where we have come from. These lessons can be modified and applied to the current times, for we know these lands have done it before, for centuries. But, the only thing that requires here is 'Conviction' and if every country starts working on building these capacities, they becoming developed economies is just a matter of time!

● Climate change will impact developed countries to continue develop

Why does climate change impact developed countries to continue develop more easily? It is one natural environment hurt problem , due to human,e.g. businessmen their damage our global natural environment behaviors, to cause any one developed countries may become developing countries in future one day in possible. I shal indicate the reasons as below:

The effects of climate change will not be uniformly distributed across the globe and there are likely to be winners and losers as the planet warms. Applying a broad brush to climate effects, developing countries are more likely to disproportionately experience the negative effects of global warming. Not only do many developing countries have naturally warmer climates than those in the developed world, they also rely more heavily on climate sensitive sectors such as agriculture, forestry and tourism. As temperatures rise further, regions such as Africa will face declining crop yields and will struggle to produce sufficient food for domestic consumption, whilst their major exports will likely fall in volume. This effect will be made worse for these regions if developed countries are able to offset the fall in agricultural output with new sources, potentially from their own domestic economies as their land becomes more suitable for growing crops. Moreover, developing countries may also be less likely to create drought resistant harvests given the lack of research funding.

Wild weather weighs on economies

The increased frequency and severity of extreme weather will weigh on government budgets. The aftermath of natural disasters often falls on authorities who are forced to spend vast amounts on clear-up operations and healthcare costs that come with experiencing extreme weather. Revenue reductions may also be experienced by countries heavily dependent on tourism or on selling fishing rights, fo

The effects on negative environment influence to developed countries and developing countries

As developed countries face an increasing strain on domestic budgets, fewer resources in the form of aid and economic development funds will flow to developing countries. The governments of these nations will be forced to channel resources away from productive and growth-enhancing projects towards countering the costs of extreme weather. Such effects will damage near-term growth prospects. Furthermore, developing countries are likely to have less capacity to rebuild. The time required to recover from natural disasters will be prolonged and if longer than the frequency in which such disasters occur, many developing economies could remain in a constant state of reconstruction.

Africa and Asia most at risk

Highly vulnerable regions in the emerging world include Sub-Saharan Africa and South and South East Asia, according to the World Bank. In South Asia, cities such as Kolkata and Mumbai will face increased flooding, warming temperatures and intense cyclones. Loss of snow melt from the Himalayas will also reduce the flow of water into the Indus Ganges and Brahmaputra basins. Meanwhile in South East Asia, Vietnam's Mekong Delta, which produces most of the rice, is especially vulnerable to rising sea levels. For Sub-Saharan Africa, food security will be a major challenge due to droughts and shifts in rainfall. Many developing nations are situated in low latitude countries and it is estimated that 80% of the damage from climate change may be concentrated. Consequently, higher agricultural yields, lower heating requirements and lower winter mortality rates are a handful of economic benefits climate change may bring, although these benefits may diminish as warming continues.

However, the prediction that developing countries will be disproportionately affected is reinforced by Standard and Poor's research on the influence climate change will have on sovereign risk. Recognising that climate change is a global mega-trend impacting sovereign risk through economic, fiscal and external performance, they find that lower-rated sovereigns appear most exposed. Based on these measures we can interpret the results in part as the susceptibility of an economy to climate change.

How poor climate change influences UK developed growth

In the UK, the average temperature is now 1°C higher that it was 100 years ago and 0.5°C higher than it was in the 1970s. As a higher latitude country, it is believed that the UK will fare better than many developing nations as global warming progresses. That is not to say the nation will escape the costs of climate change - particularly given its significant coastline where rising sea levels pose an obvious threat. According to scientists estimate of the cost of floods to the UK economy as a result of 3°C - 4°C of warming are in the region of 0.2% - 0.4% of GDP annually by the middle of the century, if flood management efforts are not strengthened.

In England, the south and parts of Yorkshire and Humberside are forecast to experience the greatest impact from flooding by 2050 . Aside from increased flooding, water availability will become progressively more constrained and droughts more frequent .Milder winters and the associated decline in cold-related mortality rates will be countered by a greater prevalence and severity of heat waves, bringing with it a higher number of heat-related mortalities. Finally, with the agricultural sector contributing approximately just 0.6% of GDP, the benefits of longer growing seasons will be marginal to the economy. In conclusion, climate change may also indirectly affect the UK economy through global supply chains. The UK may both export to and import from climate-sensitive countries. The subsequent influence of climate change in these economies may feed through to the domestic economy through lower demand for exports or higher prices of imports.

CHAPTER V

Factors Influence Human Future High Technological Development Failure

Why do developed countries need to improve on culture, education, medical technologyl development aspects?
I shall attempt to explain that why America, Japan, England and India these four countries ought need to improve on above sevearal aspects as below:
Firstly, I shall explain that why Japan still needs to improve itself country technology development, although Japan had been a technological mature development country in long time. In Japan technological development history, Japan had owned high technological development on technological products manufacture aspect, such as electronic rice cookers, artificial intelligent rice cookers cars, televisions etcl technological products. But when Germany had also began to develop high technological products in global technological prodict market. In basic, all any similar Japan technological products. Germany had also owned high technological skills to manufacture to sell in global high technological products marekt.
So, nowadays, Germany may still be Japan's high technological product main competitor. It means that global homeholders technology products consumers, car buyers must choose any Germany and Japan high technological products to compare which are better quality in order to satisfy their useful need.s Hence, in global high technological products market, Japan won't be still high technological product leader as past history. If Japan did

not continue to improve its technology, Germany will be the future high technology product leader to replace Japan, hence Japan can not neglect to consider how to continue to improve its technology development.

IN the past, science and technology in Japan is focused in vehicle manufacture technology, consumer electronic, robotics, medical devices, space exploration and film industry. For example, Japan's focus on intensive mathematics education and the reverence for engineers in Japanese culture aids enginnering talent development which as produced advances in automative engines, television display technology, videogames , optical clocks etc. On aerospace exploration aspect Japan had conducted space and planetary research., aviation research and development of space and satellites. On nuclear power development technology, since 1973, Japan has been looking to become less dependent on imported fuel and start on depend on nuclear energy. On electronic development aspect, Japan is well known for its electronic industry throughout the world, and Japanese electronic products account ofr a large share in the world market. However, Japan had beed a leading nation in scientific research, particularly biomedical research.

However, all of above technology, Germany will own advance technology to replace Japan to develop its products to sell to global easily. Germany had innovated its technology, e.g. the self -driving cars of the near future depend on precise digital geolocation data to navigate to arrive at destinations. So, Germany's non-manual driving vehicles innovation may be future nay countries car users' suppliers. Also, its battery technology is also one of future high technology mission 2021. Germany government began to support the construction of autonomous capacities in battery cell production to secure technological maximally exploit the battery calue chain. Germany government should continue to support electronic battery cell manufacturers, to drive force in the growing market for electronic cars and the goals of continuing to build their motors in Germany in the future.

Is Germany technology advanced? I believe that it is true, in the index's eighth edition for 2020, Germany was named the most technologically advanced nation, followed by South Korea, and Singapore, Germany is most known for its engineering, different high technological invention etc. aspect. Why is Germany so technologically advanced? Because Germany had been an academic powerhouse for a long time and as such education is focused on technological aspect. It's education goal is for good ideas to be translated quickly into innovative products and services. Moreover, Germany also considers Hyper automation, the distributed cloud, technological development. Some technological leaders predict the future high technological development countries may include: China, South Korea, United States , Singapre , United Kingdom, Russia, Japan and Germany .

The possible number or rank technological development countries rank may be 1 South Korea rank 2 ,ay be United States, rank 3 may be Japan, rank 4 may be Sweden nowadays. However, Germany may be future rank 1 technological leader, because Germany is so good at engineering. Germany's engineers borne out of the country are world leaders in their field, reowned for their dedication to precision, function and power. Over the years, Germany engineers have maintained their reputation to help Germany technology development products to as a top exporter of machinery and industrial equipment.

Moreover, in human development history, Germany are

smart, when Germans are the most intelligent people in Europe, the British have an edge over rivals in France when it comes to the grwy matter , a new league of IQ scores has shown. The scored 94 and Germans were tap of the table with an IQ of 107, according to Richard Lynn, who headed the study. However, why is German technology will be the best. The major factor for Germany's success is that it has managed to homegrown scientific research and expertise to move up the technological ladder, concentrating on innovative products and processes not easily copied or undercut by cheap wages. The textile industry is a case in point, hence it causes that future Germany's technology development may be Japan's future one main competitos in technological product development market. So, it is right time, Japan needs to continue to research its new technological invention in order to improve its technological development to be the best to compare other high technological development countries.

Secondly, I shall discuss that why US needs to improve or change itself country's culture to let many different countries people can adopt to live. For example, nowadays, COVID 19 illness is serious to influence any one country people live. IN fact, US ia a developed country, it is global countries only one leader to encourage different countries people to live. Also, US is one comfortable living people to let global immigrants to feel. But, when COVID 19 disease occurred, some US people feel that it is possible due to Chinese people , they contact COVID 19 disease to cause many US people get this kind of disease. However, it is none evidence to prove this kind of illness may be caused by Chiese to cause many US people die. So, US, opening culture began to change worse, e.g. some US people began to hate overseas immigrants to live itself country, it is possible due to many US people feel afraid to contact overseas immigrants, they may bring COVID 19 disease in their bodies, so when US people they contact these overseas COVID 19 disease immigrants, they may get this kind of disease . SO, it seems that US people's opening accept to let overseas immigrant living policy has changed to prohibit them to immigrate to live US easily.

However, I feel that US 's closing culture mind can not bring its social development to improve more easily. US ought to change its social culture has more opening cultural mind as before how it accepted different countries immigrants to choose US to live. Hence, it brings this question: What challenges US may encounter if it can be change its new cultural mind to accept more overseas immigrants to live easily? The challenges may include: American needs to understand themselves value and learn about what is important to Americans know why Americans value independence, equality and being on time. Americans will need see they are direct and informal and why competition, work ethic, and buying things are important in the US. American probably had strong traditions and culture that they valued. In the UNited States, there are also important American values are the things that are most important to Americans. For example, one of the main American values is independence. Independence is sometimes referred to US individualism. Americans are very proud of being self reliant, or being able to take care of themselves. American children tend to leave the home earlier than in oterh cultures, if they continue to live at home, they might be asked to pay rent or contribute to the house. So, Americans expect anyone who is able to work to do in order to support themselves. Also, Americans value privacy and their own space, when in some cultures wanting privacy may be seen as a bad thing, many Americans like to have alone time and may be private abour certain topic. In conversations, many Americans are private about certain things and do not want to talk about them, such as age, how much money they make, or their political, sexual and religious views. Americans often give each other more space in public situations than people in other cultures . They tend to stand with a bit of space between them, typically the distance of direct. This means that they often tell you what they think and they will be assertive about when they want.

Some peoples of American-style directness,, such as in conversation, if an American disagrees with youropinion, they might tell you, this does not mean they do not like you, just that they may have a different area. In classes, Americans may challenge their teachers' ideas. IN some culture, it is impolite to disagree with your teacher, it is never is rude to ask for help. Most Americans love to help and need very little encouragement to become good friends and neighbors.

However, I feel that America has lose equality value. Although, many newly immigrants moved to America to follow American team. They believed that if you worked hard, you could move up in society. But, today, more and more people realize the American dream is not true. Many people who work very hard do not have very much money. Often people who love from privileged backgrounds have an easier time moving up in the world. Still, the idea of equality is an important part of US culture.

So, COVID 19 disease occurrence had explained that US began have inequality culture difference causes, discrimination to overseas immigrants, e.g. Chinese. Americans discrimination behavior began to cause.

American ought change itself new culture to traditional culture to accept different countires clever immigrants skills, talent people mind in order to help itself country to continue develop more advanced society to be world leader position.

Thirdly, I shall discuess why England needs to improve education. What negative impacts will happen, if UK does not continur improve education as well as its neglect on improvement education, how it will bring negative impact to its studetns minds in society? Why growth is the key to improve UK education development? Conventional wisdom states that smaller schools provide students with a better education . But studies of education systems around the world, show that growing schools could actually solve UK's poor student outcomes.

Nowadays, the UK's school system is in trouble, despite the fact that the last two decades have seen massive changes in the UK's education sector. UK education report indicated that in the past 15 years, the UK's four countries have spent $550 UK billion on operating and enhancing their secondary schools. IN the same period, England alone closed 35% of its schools (1,500 institutions) and opened almost 2,000 new ones . Nonetheless, little has improved UK education report indicated that in 2026, only 65% of all English pupils graduated with five or more grade as compared with 50% 15 years ago, at a cost od $37 billion per percentage point of improvement. The US was as a wholw spent the 8 th largest amount of 34 OECD countries, but only came, 19 th in mathemactics, 16 th in reading and 14 th in science.

So, what 's going wrong to cause UK students have worse learning performance. The reasons may include: Neglecting all four nations education reforming. Education in the UK is devolved to the four nations that make up the British union. For this reason, most of qualifications data relates only to England, although total spending figures are mostly UK wide. Academy shcools are amodel of schooling that is available only in England. There is no provision for the model in the other three nations of the UK.

The next reason is failure educational strategy. UK education report also indicated that England's strategy over the past 15 years has been to try to improve its education system by fixing its low lights , less than a third of students graduate with five or more GCE grade , reducing their projected lifetime earnings by $140,000. By putting their schools into " special measures" and offering them up for tender to other schools, it hopes that whole education system would improve. BUt, it has not . THe English have thrown more money at the proble,, spending 84% more on each child's education . Then, they did 15 years ago ($57,000 rather than $31,000), but although half their schools have improved, the other half have declined, and the overall picture is still the same. So, there are still many UK schools can not get UK government help to improve all school students individual learning effort to be better.

- What would have happened if UK government had spent the last 15 years trying to grow their education system bright lights, rather than brighten , their low lights? UK education improvement strategy is such that a similar change in strategy helped the charity save the children reduce malutrition by 80% in Vietnam over two years, after decades of getting. Instead of trying to solve the poor learning ability of student learning performing problems in their worst areas, UK educators also need to expand a similar improvement education on strategy shift in order to help transform to UK any schools reforming educational

policies in success.
Hence, if England had adopted another long term countrywide educational strategy, where all schools work together to improve standards across the UK in order to access all schoools resources, facilities and entracurricular activities and it could shown that good teachers in both schools can teach anyone. Then, most of UK teachers can know their subject inside out and quickly adapt their teaching methods to different needs. Consequently, when UK can imporve most of UK students learning effort to the best performance, as better educated students are more knowledgeable, money when they can attribute their the best effort to their society in the future. Then, UK society can be developed to reach the most top level, because UK's future development must depend on its next generation's help. If future UK education can train many talent students to attribute to social different aspects, such as technology, medical , business, construction etc. different professional aspects . UK future social development may be improved to be better to compare present society development. So, UK government can not neglect how to improve all UK student individual learning performance in order to help every UK student to pursuc thcir abilities to prepare to attribute to UK future society devleopment successfully.
Finally, I shall discuss why India will need to improve medical technology. Recently, world news reported that INdia has many people are killed by COVID 19 disease. India is the highest population country. I assume that COVID 19 disease causes many Indians die because India has no enough hospitals, clinics to provide good medical quality to serve these COVID 19 disease contact patients. Due to lack of the best medical skillful doctors and nurses. So, many COVID 19 disease patients can not be saved to

their lifes, even in India society, many none of COVID 19 disease contact people, when they contact to the COVID 19 disease people, they can not give good drugs to save themselves lifes. SO, it explains why India has many people are killed by COVID 19 disease in short time . SO, it seems that India lacks enough drugs to supply to these COVID 19 disease patients to cause there are many COVID 19 disease patients die in short time.

This COVID 19 diease attracks India matter occurs, it brings these questions: IS short time shortage of drug supply factor or long time shortage of drug supply factor to cause many COVID 19 disease patients die? Can long time poor medical technology factor cause many Indians die? IS COVID 29 disease the main factor causes many Indians die? India has many people are living. So, India must eed to improve its medical technology in order to solve the number increasing of India people future health challenge. One of the most important and highly debated, elements of India society is the quality of healthcare available to patients. The use of technology increases provider capability and patient access when improving the quality of life for some India clients and saving the lives of others. The India technology role can play in improving health of India. It can help in early detection of health problems. It cn also help in data collected from tests instantly monitor, the conditon of the patient, and then relay that information to the doctors and staff of the overall healthcare system.

However, the factors have made improvement in health conditions possible in India , they may include: A downtrend in communicable diseases, a focus on prevention , reduced neonatal mortality rates, tacking antimicrobial resistance, improved nutrition, using digital health and artificial intelligence for social impact, stronger government accountability. A number of industry analysts have observed that increased accessibility of treatment is one of the most tangible ways that technology has changed healthcase. Health IT opens up may more avenues of exploration and research, which allows experts make helathcare more driven and effectve than it has ever been. Hence, future India may apply these new medical technology, e.g. virtual reality, precision medicine, health wearables, artificial organs, 3D printing, wireless brain sensors, robotic surgery, smart inhalers, they are the main treatment option for asthma and if taken correctly, will be effective for 80% of India patients.

Hence, India must need solve medical technology improvement challenge in order to keep many people lifes , in special for the talent youngers, e.g. doctors, scientists, architects, lawyers, accountants , atc. professionals. I believe that India's medical technology can not been improved to raise quality in order to save many COVID 19 disease patents their lifes. So, many of COVID 19 disease patients can not been saved by good quality if medical drugs in short time. So, if INdia does not hope to lose many young talent professionals, it must need to continue improve its medical technology as soon as possible.

● How can our future social development can be improved ?

Nowadays, globalization cooperation or our societies become one society to any countries leaders is needed. I believe that countries competition will be serious, even we shall attack other countries if any one country can not accept " globalization cooperation mind". I mean that it is only globalization cooperation one way choice, then our societies can be improved or will be become better more easily.

For China and America two countries example, recently, because COVID 19 disease caused many Western and Asia countries began feel that COVID 19 disease was caused from Chinese. However, they have no evidence to indicate that COVID 19 disease must be caused from China. Although, before the year end of two years, there are some Chinese had ever travelers to US, then US had many people began to get this kind COVID 19 disease to cause many American die, when they did not believe that COVID 19 disease can cause human dies easily. Until to now, global many people had gotten this kind of illness to vause they die, when the health person contacts the owned COIVD 19 disease sick people . Although some people can be saved after they are saved by drug, but many people can not be saved, when they can not been saved by drug, even they still can not saved after they had been gotten drug. Such as US, UK, India, China, Germany , Korea, Japan, France these countries reported that they had many people could not saved to keep their lifes when they could not believe that they can get COVID 19 disease when they contact to the strange people who may owned COVID 19 diesease easily, when they are sitting down to the same table to eat in restaurants or when the COVID 19 disease strange person and the health person are talking together closely.

So, I believe that it is right time to any countries leaders need to act and to cooperate to find the method to avoid COVID 19 disease attacks any people. I mean the globalization cooperation attitude may nee to ourselves countries leaders . Our country leader can not only consider himself/herself country benefit and neglact to consider other countries benefits. If global humans hope that we can still to improve our culture to be peace or improve our space technology artificial intelligent development manufacturing to the advance level rapidly, or improve our medical technology to the best quality or improve our students learning effort or teachers teaching performance to reach the most satisfactory need to our future any one students. It is only global cooperation way to achieve global improved societies aim. If our societies or any one country leader still only consider how to protect himself/herself country businessmen benefits and leader himself/herself benefits, and rich people benefits , but they neglect to consider any one citizen benefits ,e.g. the low education, poor old age people, low income people in societies.Then, unfair and discrimination will be encouraged to occur in any one country society . Consequently when any one country low education , low income , poor old people can not feel comfortable to lieve in themselves countries. They will feel angry to complain themselves countries governments and leader individual ambitious behavior to influence these group people feel unhappy to live long time in themselves countries.

Consequently, the country's social education level will only continue to worse, even economy will continue recession, as ell as and kind of technologies won't continue improve. Due to our future any one country leader can not keep globalization cooperation mind or positive opening attitude to let any one itself country citizen feels comfortable to live forever. Then, the developed country ,e g. US, UK will not still keep technology development leading position easily. It is possible due to they only consider themselves social benefits, during this COVID 19 disease had been attacking themselves countries. So, they ought also consider other countries , they are attacked by COVID 19 disease, hoe to avoid COVID 19 disease will continue to attack any one country easily.

Hence, we only cooperate to help ourselves to find the best long time method to fight COVID 19 disease . When our countries leaders can cooperate to spend time to sit down to discuss how to fight COVID 19 disease , then I believe that our global societies may been improved more better rapidly as soon as possible in this year.

● Methods to avoid future human developmend failure

Finally, I shall conclude that how we can avoid human development failure. we need to know that human is facing threat of self-benefit behavior. We can follow our development to analyze why we shall encounter failure of improvement stage in our soon future. In our past thousand years, human had developed in success from fishing, agriculture stage till to manufacture industry innovation stage, till to nowadays high technological development stage ,even our future artificial intelligent high technology (non-manual control machine stage). Although all of our past development , till to nowadays development, it seems that we can develop in success in any technological aspects ,e.g. space, computer , internet , ecommerce , medical technology etc. even future non-manual control (AI) artificial intelligent technology. But, some ways may help us to continue high technological development in success, even damage our future continue high technological development. They may include unfriend or poor culture development, lacking globalization cooperation, self -beefit mind factors.

All of above factors are any countries leades self-benefit mind or negative attitude (human behavior) to influence our future high technology continue development can succeed in possible. The reason is because that if any one country leader only considers how to protect himself/ herself country technological development beefit, it means that he/she does not allow his/her country talent scientists can discess their any new technological invention opinions to let other countries talent scientists to learn ho to improve themselves new technological invention together. This point is the main bad factor to cause human future any kinds of high technological development to delay in possible, because our any kinds of high technological development success, we must depend on global scientists can have chance to share their any kinds of new technological experiments to let they can learn why the scientist can develop the kind of product in success, or why the scientist can not develop the kind of product in success. Then, any one country scientists can absorb other countries scientists their successful or failure scientific experiements in order to improve their any kinds of new technological expeiment to achieve the most satisfactory scientific experiement demand to bring benefit to us. So, globalization cooperation is the only way to avoid human development failure absolutely.

● Why do developed countries need to continue to learn how to improve new technology ?

In fact, there are different between developing and developed countrics. Dcvcloping countries, such as Afria, Korea, China, Taiwan, these countries are developing, so their IT information , medical, manufacturing technology, artificial intelligence etc. different industries are not mature, they must need to continue improvement to develop their skills in order to satisfy consumers market need. Because social need had been often changing, so these developing countries scientists, businessmen need to have good learning mind to prepare to learn how technological , medical , artificial intelligent, IT knowledge in order to satisfy consumer individual new product useful need and keep market competitive effort in themselves home an overseas consumption markets both more easilu. But, why do developed countries also need to continue to learn how to improve new technology? What negative impacts will bring to developed countries their scientists and businessmen do not continue to improve their new products development or continue to research how to improve their old products to achieve the best quality to order consumers needs.

Nowadays, global consumption market competition is serious. Consumer individual need or demand is increasing, when one consumer feels the kind of old product can not satisfy his/her actual need, he/she will seek to find which brands of products, they have similar function or useful characteristics in order to make comparison to other similar kinds of products. Then, he/she will make final purchase decision. So, when the consumer had habit to use the brand of product, it does not mean that he/she will continue to use this brand of product. He/she may be influenced to change to choose the another brand of similar function characteristics of new product to buy use in this rapid changing competitive market.

Hence, if the developed country's culture is changed to closing mind from opening mind. These developed country, such as US people can not accept to other countries people new, useful, attributing innovativ mind of ideas easily. They only consider or recognite that themselves ideas are the best or the most useful. Consequently, due to their foolish closing minds, their traditional protection themselves believes will cause difficult to continue to improve or develop, because it is possible that there are any other developed countries, e.g.

UK, Germany, Japan, they have some talent people, scientists their technological skills may be proficient or more advanced to compare US, itself countries some scientists.

So, I recommend that any developed countries can not only consider to appreciate themselves countries scientists must be the most smart to compare other developed countries. Any one developed country scientists ought need to cooperate with other developed countries scientists to discuss or research any new invention together in order to help themselves technology can been improved rapidly in order invent many different kinds of new products to satisfy consumers themselves often changing useful needs in this global consumption market nowadays.

This developed country Japn is one good example to explain that why its scientists ought need to continue to improve their different technology or science skills as well as learn any new kinds of technology or science knowledge from other developed countries scientists , such as US, UK, Germany together. Because it is only one effective technology and science improvement method (way) to Japan scientists,when they can accept the other developed scientists different new or innovated opinions as well as they can spend some time to sit down to discuss and cooperate to help themselves old products how to change or innovate new products in order to attract global consumers purchase choice. So, although, Japan had been one developed country long time, its technology development had searched mature stage in the past, But, it can not reprsent that its technology must be more advanced to compare other developed countries, such as UK, US, Germany. Because these any one developed country, their scientists still continue carry on researching how to improve themselves old products to be new. So, it seems that Japan's any old technological products, e.g. smart phones, television, washing machines, rice coolers, products won't bring more attract to persuade global consumers choices. Because US, UK, Germany etc. different developed countries scientists had began to research how to continue improve its traditional old technological products to be more attraction in order to adopt global technological products users needs. For example, developing country India, due to its medical technology is poot, if it hopes to improve itself country technology, it must need to attempt to concentrate on spending money, medical teaching resources on medical technology aspect. India's medical technology improvement must be any kinds of technologies , the most need to improve to compare IT technology, manufacturing technology, artificial intelligent technology, space technology etc. The reason is that India is the highest population country, if its medical technology's cost, it will cause many young talent people die, such as COVID 19 disease occurs to India recently. It causes many Young talent Indians die, due to it lasks enough good medical technology to supply drugs to save them. So, if India government hopes that it can have many talent high skillful technology youngers to serve itself country. It will need to consider how to improve its medical technology in order to fight any possible new kind of illness attack, instead of COVID 19 disease, when India can improve its medical technology to save many young talent scientists' lifes . Then, it won't lose many talent scientists and they can continue to attribute themselves scientific knowledge for India itself country lont time technological science development.

Hence, UK and US both governments need to consider how to allocate enough land to supply to any manufacturing and business operations efficiently, how to help any educational organizations to train talent employees and school organizations to teach talent students, how to supply enough loan to assist any business founders to develop their new businesses in success or create new entrepreneurship. All of these can bring advantages to satisfy their societies needs.

Economists generally agree that highly economic development and growth are influenced by four factors: Human resources, physical capital, natural resource and technology. So, in general, US an UK countries hope they can become highly developed countries have government that focus on these areas. They mean that factors may influence one developed country to continue to become highly developed country, factors may include: accumulation of capital stock, increases in talent labor inputs, such as workers or hour worked, technological advancement. All of these factors may assist UK , US continue to bring highly development benefit. So, UK, US are such as industrialization in developed countries, they need to improve these industrial productivity in order to continue to keep, highly developed countries in possible, these factors may include: long term technological development, improvement quality of human resources, encough availability of finace, efficient managerial talent, efficient government policy and surplus of enough supply of natural factor, e.g. good climate for agriculture, enough natural coal , land natural resource supply. However, they also need to consider these are negative factors to affect them to continue develop, e.g. lack of drive of social motivation for improvement, unproductive social functions, such as war or having very large family sizes, negative social cultures, such as gambling and drinking wine, and lack of skills due to poor training and education . They may be poor social negative factors to influence they continue develop in success.

CHAPTER VI

Can Theater Leisure Improve Developed And Developing Countries Culture

Past, present and future theatre performance Development

- How to improve past theatre performance to be better?

Firstly, we need to know whether how our global theatre performance

feature trends. In history of theatre charts , the development of theatre over the past, these performance developed into dramas, how did theatre change over time? As we explore how the theatre has changed over the years. We can see that in some ways the theatre has changed over the years. We can see that in some ways that it did not change that much. A thousand years after the first plays more staged, people still loved bawdy, explicit comedies about society. Later in thc rcstoration period, theatres began to stage so called " machine plays".

What is the history of theatre development ? History of theatre origins of Greek theatre, i.,e. in the levels of the followers of Dionysus, a god of fertility and wine. In the 6th century BC a PRIEST OF Dionysus , by the name of Thespis introduces a new element which can validly be seen as the birth of theatre.

How did Philippine theatre change over the years? After the Japanese occupation, the Philippine theatre has evolved to become an amalgamation of the3 various influences, such that of the Zarzela, comedia, Western classics etc. performances. By the 1950s, theatre had moved out of classrooms and the3 concept of paying for a ticket to see a theatrical performance emerged.

- What are the three origins of theatre development ?

The theatre of ancient Greece consisted of three types of drama:

Tragedy, comedy and Satyr play. The origins of theatre in ancient Greece , according to Arisotle (384 B322 BCE), theatre , are to be found in the festivals. Hence, our nowadays theatre performance is the evolution of modern theatrical production , we take a look at how the theatre has evolved over the year. In the past, theatre had been a welcome distraction. Trim tragedy, comedy, and satyr play performance mainly. In many locations, theatre as performance evolved from other ideas, such as old Roman philosopher , statue. Traditional theatre performance had been developed to today's digital performances in past forms of theatrical technology, due to theatre performance audience visual leisure needs (demand) had been changing.

- What makes a good theatre performance?

Today, theatre performance had been influenced by audience visual leisure changing need. A great theatre performance is one where the characters are compelling . The characters will be the most recognized part of the theatre performance. They arte the people that act out the pitot and deal with the conflict and problems of the plot. The audience will mostly be interested in learning more about the character.

What is a performance in theatre? In performing, acts, a performance generally comprises , an event in which a performer, or group of performers, present one or more works of act to an audience. In instrumental music and drama , a performance is typically described as a " play" . A performance also describes the way in which an actor performs.

What is modern theatre feature? Modern theatre also known as 20th century theatre, impacting Asian, European and American theatre forms. It focused on a board perception of looking in to art, including theatre, critically, e.g. realism, musical theatre, opera are forms on new theatres.

Thus, theatre for development is a type of community-based or it is very important for actors and organizers of the performance or performance project. For example, theatre for positive youth development, theatre teacher needs to educate students how they see performance, which can bring positive social emotional to feel whether the theatre to let audiences to know. So, nowadays, theatre performance is needed to develop through drama. Theatre performance needs to provide visual leisure and education both aims, e.g. theatre actors and performance producers need to learn how to produce and inspire exciting and imaginative theatre, they aim to learn how to provide professional theatre performance production, education and training and visual leisure act performance development aspects, during the performance , the audience was asked what the actors reflected present community concerns and attitudes. A lot of work goes into creating a theatre performance. Today, theatres can generally be divided into two types: Producing theatres or leisure theatres. Producing theatres have creative teams which develop new productions from existing or new work, otherwise, leisure theatre aims to produce any kinds of visual leisure performance aim.

● Future theatre performance ought how to develop?

Future theatre performance tends on technology, scenographic performance, communal argument reality and the future of theatre and performance development and proposed how these might influence and benefit the development of theatre acts and lives, dramatic performance ,e.g. live performance theatres., they will continue to develop on appreciation for in-person experiences.

In the last few years, technological development likes virtual reality theatre and performance will be developed in their own visual leisure unique performance features to let audiences feel the different visual leisure enjoyment by technology performance improvement, e.g. smaller theatres can benefit from a wide range of societal theatres and develop it themselves . Also, in Western country, US , it tends to develop professional non-for-profit theatre field. In development a child's ability to understand the lives of others and fostering a deepe3r sense of compassion. Moreover, the future theatre artistic voice through the experience of live performance.

● How does technology transfer stage performance?

Other kind of future theatre performance development is digital development in theatre. In theatre om audiences ,which will use their experience in theatre and performance on the digital music performance and video performance theatres both aspects. Future theatre industry will be experimenting digital performance. The future of theatre and stage performance is setting up digital kind of leisure performance, it may include: Venue planning, auditorium, seating design, digital performance production, specialist architectural lighting and performance sound, digital platform for the acts. If you are an individual audience customer, you will be influenced to choose to see digital theatre performance more than traditional tool to provide the act students with an in depth view of performances of essential. Rather than considering the real time or temporality of events, digital theatre concerns the interactions of people (audience and actors) sharing the same physical space (in an least one location, if multiple audiences exists).

The first digital theatre is founded in 2009, digital theatre is already the world's leading educational the world's leading educational platform for the performing acts. Today, digital theatres can provide 3 million students in over 2000 schools, colleges and universities across 65 counties with unlimited access to over 1,000 more full length productions and educational resources. However, digital theatre has provided free access to its archive of performances, it had been announced by their accounts managers.

IN the future, any one can watch digital theatre, we can watch digital performance on TV, desktop, tablet and mobile. Screen mirroring via a chromecast dongle from audience mobile or laptop. So, digital theatre can provide any audiences to watch performances in any places. It is a " live" performance placing at least some performers in the same shared physical space with an audience. Hence, digital theatre enriches and enhances the experience of watching a performance with exclusive . So, digital performances have the potential to open up access to the theatre to much wider population, when COVID 19 disease impacts theatres can nor permit open to let many people sit together in theatres. So, virtual performances can help theatres to keep functioning in lockdown or when outdoor performance. So , theatre and performance in digital culture examines the recent history of advanced technologies, including new performance leisure digital media. It will be accepted to watch an performance from desktop , laptop, mobile etc. technological performance platforms in the world.

What performance skills to future theatre performance individual need

- What are theatrical skills?

The performing arts primarily focus on dance, drama, music and theatre. This means there's often overlap with the film. However, the skills that performer needs to be a performance artist. They may include: confidence, the ability to network and market the performer himself/ herself , self -discipline, on analytical mind the ability to self-reflect, flexibility , teamwork , organization and the management personal characteristics.

To develop a range of physical skills and techniques, e.g. movement, body language , posture, feature, coordination, timing, control, facial expression, eye contract, listening, expression of mood, awareness, interaction with other performers, dance and choral movement. Thus, performance skills are goal directed actions that a person enacts when performing a task. Focusing on performance skill is what makes occupational therapy's contribution to unique and powerful . Thus, making a good theatre performance , a great theatre performance is one where the characters one compelling. The characters will be the recognized part of the theatre performance. They are the people that act the plot and deal with the conflicts of and problems of the pilot. Also talent and technology is the most important skill to influence any one performer whose theatre music , dance, stage entertainment.

What are some life skills that are used I theatre? Life skills learned in theatre may include : Oral communication skills, creative problem solving abilities, motivation and commitment, willing to work cooperatively, the ability to work independently, time-budget skill. So, it implies that performer individual needs to learn right life skill and like attitude in order to achieve the excellent performances. Theatre performance ought have relationship to any one performer life experience. So., life experience is also one important factor to influence any one theatre performer's performance can bring more attractive or not to satisfy any audience's leisure need. Moreover, another kind acting skills are also important to influence theatre performance. Acting involves a board range of skills, including a well-developed imagination, of speech and the ability to interpret drama.

Another kind acting skills are also important factor to influence any one theatre performer's performance can bring more attration or not to satisfy any audience 's leisure need. Moreover, acting involves a board range of skills, including a well developed imagination, emotional facility , physical expressivity, vocal projection , kind clarity of speech and the ability to inteerpret drama, another kind is performance skills, performance skills are goal-directed actions that a person enacts when performing a task. It causes on performance skill is what makes occupational therapy's contribution to unique and powerful.

- main elements influences theatre performance

Thus, to achieve the best theatre performance objective, the three basic elements of theatre may include : performers, audience , director, theatre space, design aspects (scenery, costume, lighting and sound), text which includes focus purpose point of view. However, the most important life skill , any one performer needs to learn in theatre is communication. Many theatre performers develop the ability to speak clearly, incidly and thoughtfully . When the performer acts on stage , he is comfortable speaking to range groups of people. Many theatre companies look for this in an individual when individuals who can demonstrate excellent verbal and written communication skills, teamwork, and attraction performing actions in order to satisfy audience leisure need, when they decide to buy ticket to see the theatre performance show.

Thus, when a theatre student hopes to learn theatre skills easily or understands easily. He/she ought have these psychologicall attitufes: Self awarenesses, being open and receptive to criticism, teamwork, time management, dealing with all types of different people, confidence and public speaking skills, being realistic. He also needs to know whether he ought how to learn theatre acting, such as learn to use masterclass, read actor biographies or autobiographics, be more abservant of people in action, listen to podcasts, teach others, study people who are like what skills the perfrmer can learn from drama. Drama promotes communicataion skills, teamwork,dialogue, negotiation, socialization. It stimulates th imagination and creativity. It also develops a better understanding of human behavior and empathy with situations that might seem distant. Performance skills in drama may include: movement-soft, gentle, heavy light , quick show, resture signals with your hands/arms to show feelings, facial expressions wide eyed, norrow eyed, raised eyebrows, troubled permanent frown, down turned mouth, eye contact staring, glaring fleeting, voice-pitch high and squeaky , low and soft etc. body language skills.

In fact, students involved in drama performanc coursework when one student decides to learn theatre performance or experience outscored non-act students. Drama can improve skills and academic performance in children and youth with learning disabilities . Because the practical role performing acts plays in a well-rounded. It's about learning transferable life skills. By observing others students learn to make creative choices on stage by creativity and imagination. So, Drama classes can give performance chance to let theatre students to attempt to improve their performing skills. Also, drama enhances students' artistic and creative abilities and gives them a better performance improvement through learning which involves thought, feeling and action, workshops and attendance at theatre performances.

On conclusion, the performing acts primarily focus on dance, drama, music and theatre perforforming acts students can develop skills needed for life and music, theatre, and speech and debate activities are ideas for them to learn through intensive research not just facts and every time performance learning courts can let they have performance practice experience to improve their next performance more attractive. Hence, every time theatre performance practice can help any theatre students to improve thwir life skills, acting skills , performance skills absolutely.

Theatre performance brings what social benefit

- Why do our society need theatre performance?

What benefits of music, drama, dance, act performance , they can bring benefits to our society? How they can impact our social future development? What negative impacts, they will influence to our social development? I shall attempt to answer these questions concern future theatre performance whether it ought continue to develop or not.

Theatre can improve social bonding, allow do emotions to be explored in a safe space, develop the emotional and cognitive skills to deal with a complicated world, and kick-start coversations about important issues. How does theatre contribute to society? The theatre , dance and other performing arts can teach people how to express themselves effectively and can also be a tool though with people with disabilities can communicate. In addition to teaching self-expression, the performing arts, help society or a whole in self-knowledge and understanding.

What is the purpose of theatre for social change? It is unlike other kind of theatre, theatre for social change is a performance to raise awareness about the impact of social issues through community engagement process. How does theatre have an economic impact on society? Theatre and performing arts are also hugely imported to economies and brings societies positive impact. The US Bureau of economic analysis showed that 3.2 % of US GDP around US$504 billions is attributable to arts and culture (compared with the entire US travel and tourism industry, which accounts for 2.8% of GDP).

Hence, in theatre performance, originally a supplemental performance by an actor or actress, who kept all or past of the theatre performance. The benefits of drama performance, the benefits are physical , emotional , social and they help to develop , health society in many cases the quality of any performance reliance on an performance.

- Threatre performance brings what beneftis to impact our future social development ?

some benefits include emotional, social , physical and even academic aspects, instead of economyic benefit to societies. What are theatre performance emotional benefit? On student theatre performance educstional aspect, a range of emotions and encourage them to understand and deal with similar feelings . They may be experiencing, aggession and tension are releases in a sage , controlled theatre performance learning environment. So, there are five benefits to students who participate in theatre arts. They may include: helping them to build empathy emotion, whe kids participate any characters playing in thetre performance. They can learn how to control emotions to keep calm more than engry feeling or emotions in any future working environment easily when they need to work in society.

Improvement academic performance, participation in drama boosts students feelings of belonging and keeps them motivated at school, building goal-setting direction mind, self-esteem. All of these positive emotions, any student may be influenced when he/she can spend time to participate any kinds of theatre performance learning chance. So, the main purpose of theatre performances i s that , in fact, the purpose of theatre is to provide through job to people. The threatre is a branch of the performing arts and it is concerned with the acting our stories in front of the audience. The benefits of performing arts include improving life skills and academic performance to students.

● How can watching theatre benefit the mind?

These who watch live theatre have a reduction of stress and tension. The experience is to immersive that the audience can quickly become in the show. Live theatre allows you to forget about your daily stresses and feel as peace when you are watching in theatre hall. Hence, the benefits of drama for children, a good understand of characters, roles and subtext of plays will allow childrens' emotional intelligence building through the use of imagination, also live performance could also provide a host of developmental benefits, including improved emotionable child,individual can also bring emotional intelligence from theatre art performance learning, it focuses students can spend how much time to participate in youth theatre and still loves to attend live performances.

What re theatre performance social benefits? community theatres involves more participants, present more performances of more. Participation in community theatre brings with it on immediate social circle, and all the networking benefits. How does theatre contribute to society? The theatre, dance and music and drama etc.performance acts can teach people to express themselves effectively, and can also be a tool through which people with disabilities can communicate . In addition to teaching self-expression, the performing arts help society as a whole in self-knowledge and understanding can theatre bring positive and/or negative social change?

Theatre for social change is one of many frameworks that can be used to solve problems and create changes in society. However, the unique part of the theatre , which utilize and engage directly with the full human body. Horeover, theatre performance can let many studetns feel that theatre helps them develop the confidence that's essential to speaking clearly, lucidly and throughfully. Acting onstage teaches students how to be comfortable speaking in front of large audiences, and some of student theate performing learn classes will give them additional experience telling to groups.

- What physical benefits can bring to individual from theatre performance?

Instead of theatre performance can bring social, economic emotion benefits to society , student individual emotion, economic income growth. Whether theatre performance can bring benefits to audiences when they buy ticket to watch any kinds of theatre performance in theatres. How can watching theatre benefit the audience individual mind? Theatre encourages and expresses emotions in their most extreme form. As a human, watching any kinds of theatre performance or listening any kinds of music performance in theatre, others express emotions can trigger that their emotion repsonse in audience individual feeing as well. Theatre shows healthy to let any one audience to feel all types of emotin and to understand empathy. So, it seems that theatre is not only entertaining, but also has both mental and physical health benefits crucial for a healthy lifestyle. When audiences who attend performing arts events are healthier, have lower anxiety, and are less likely to suffer from depression.

● Can theatre performance improve studend individual academic performance?

Can student often watch theatre performance to improve his/her academic performance? It seems that these questions concern whether watching theatre performance, which can boost academic performance. It shows that educational psychologists believe that engaging with performing arts can boost the academic performance of the average child by 4 % when drama is part of curriculum.

The social benefits of theatre and performance include better self-efficiency in children and teenagers, as well as making them better equipped to broach complex subjects. How does theatre help education? Using drama and theatre as a tool to teach is not only effective, it will also bring the necessary change in the learning process for students. This concept helps students learn better, instead of simply being observers. They get to be a part of the learning process. So, theatre can enrich, student individual life, because these it does not harm, expresses a basic human instinct, brings people together models democratic discourse, contributes to education and literary , sparks economic revitalization, and influences how we think and feel generation's learning life.

- How do the arts improve academic performance?

Student s that like a combination of arts programs demonstrate improved verbal, reading, and math skills, and also show a greater capacity for higher ordered thinking skills, such as analyzing and problem solving. How can theatre help student learning development in his/her learning living experience? Many students find that theatre helps them develop the confidence that is essential to speaking clearly and thoughfully. Acting on stage teaches student how to be comfortable speaking in front of large audiences, and some of students their theatre classes will give them additional experience talking to groups. The recent university university research explored the educational and social benefits from theatres, theatres can improve social bonding, allow for emotions to be explored in a hallpy life environment. So, students can improve their communication skills and their capacity to read -write and speak when they can attempt to spend some extra time to participate to learn theatre performance in schools.

I means that little time spending theatre performance learning participation , it can improve student individual academic performance in possible , other excess time spending theatre performance learning participation it can not improve student individual academic learning performance, even it can bring worse academic result, because busy theatre students, involved in a production or other theatre projects when also taking a heavy academic load. So, I believe that theatre performance learning participation ought improve any student individual academic performance, but it depends on whether he/she spends some extra little time to particpate any kinds of theatre learning performance or spends more time to participate any kinds of theatre learning performance. It is value research whether theatre performance how to influence academic performance on education issue aspect.

Audience choices between theatre and cinema movie leisure

- Supply and demand view to future theatre and cinema movie leisure industry

In audience behavioral leisure psychology view, when the audience consumer has time to spend watching lesiure activity. When he feels leisure time is less , he will make watching lesiure either he makes purcahse ticket decision to enter cinema to watch movie or he makes purchase ticket decision to enter theatre to watch art performance, So, it seems that any kinds of movie may be any kinds of art performance competitors. Howwver, those factors may influence theatre performance audience number, they may include whether that art performance is attractive to satisfy audience's visual leisure feelingl, how many movies number is supplied to cinemas or how many art performance number is supplied to theatres, how many audiences number choice to buy ticket to watch art performance or, watch movie.

So, it implies that movie number may influence theatre art performance audiences number because watching leisure audiences may watch any kinds of movies or theatre performances. In supply and demand view , it explains when the consumer feels watching leisure need in any holiday, he needs either to watch the movie or watch the theatre performance. Hence, whether the month has how many movies have already been watched by audiences in cinemas. Their movies number may absolute influence theatre performance audiences choice to watch which movie in order to replace any one theatre performance.

Hence, any one theatre performance provider, whose competitors may include other theatre performance providers and other movie providers both , even online theatre performaners, because any one audience may choose to watch art performance from internet channel. Hence, future theatre performance market competition is serious. I believe that instead of whether the theatre performance arrangement is attractive factor, ticket price is resonable factor, performance time factor, the theatre design facility factor may also influence audiences wathing to the theatre performance choice.

It means that theatre facility environment may be one influential factor to persuade audiences to enter the theatre to watch the art performances. If the theatre facility environment light and sound facilities are not supplied enough to satisfy audience 's listening and watching feeling. They can not sit comfortable in the theatre seats. Any of these external theatre environment facility factor also may influence audiences number to the threatre. So, future theatre environment facilities must be needed to raise quality in order to achieve the high service enjoyable level to satisfy audiences leisure need, e.g. electronic moving seats, they can let audiences have auto rising or fallig feeling when they are still sitting on the seat in theatres. Music must need soft music, it can not permit loud in theatre environment, because soft music can let audiences to feel comfortable to watch and listen any kind of art performance. The art performance time can not perform too short time, e.g. half hour, but performance time can not be long time, e.g. more than two hours, because the art performance time is too short , it will let audiences feel ticket price is too high, but if the art performance time is too long, it will let audiences feel boring when they need spend long time to sit on seats.

Hence, any one art performance time is also one important factor to influence audience individual leisure feeling. Moreover, any kinds of theatre art performance must need have educational aim. It means that the art performers must need to let students feel that they can learn knowledge to be applied to their life experiences after they watched the art performance, because nowadays, many audiences are young, they choose to watch the kind of art performance, they need have leisure feeling and learning new life experience knowledge from the kind of art performance, because some young people choose to watch the kind of art performance, they hope to learn new life experience knowledge in order to pursue art performance career.

So, whether the art performance can let th young student to feel that he can learn art performance skills or not, it will influence the art performance learner to choose to watch the kind of art performance or not. Hence, whether the kind of art performance, it has educational feelingto the art performance learning audience, it will influence whether the art performance learner to choose to go to theatre to watch the art performers; performance in theatre, because if the art performance learners feel the kind of art performance can not let them to feel they can learn any new art performance skill, they won't choose to buy ticket to watch the kind of art performance. So, any one art performance provider must need to consider performance leisure and performance educational both aims in order to satisfy art performance lesiure audiences and art

performance learner audiences their psychological needs.
In fact, instead of lesiure art performance audiences, learning art performance, they will be another main audiences source, such as art performance students, because they need to go to classroom to listen art performance teachers to learn any kinds of art performance skill, they also choose to buy ticket to watch any kinds of art performance because watching art performance may be another kind of learning art performance skillful method to raise improve their art performance skills, So , future art performers need to know how to perform in order to satisfy art performance student individual learning need. So,, future any art performance students may be any one art performance service provider 's audiences. They can not neglect this new art performance student audience group in future art performance market development trend.
On conclusion, when art performance students feel the kind of art performance can satisfy their art performance skill learning need. They won't choose spend much time to buy ticket to enter cinemas to watch movies, even if the kind of art performance service leisure provider can provide any kinds of attractive art performance to let audiences to watch, as well as the theatre facilities can be improved more comfortable feeling, then many movie audiences will be persuaded to buy ticket to enter theatres to watch any kinds of art performances.
So, future theatre performance market development success depends on art performer individual performance skill, theatre facilities service improvement, art performance ticket price and performance time factors. Also, the difference between movie performancers and art performancers is that movie performaners can not do "life show". Otherwise, art performancers can do life show, life

show is one kind of life experience, every art performer needs to do life experience, perform on theatre, they can have immediate emotion feeling from audiences whether they like their art performance or they dislike their art performance. When they are performing life show in theatre.So, their satisfactory feeling ought be more than movie performers. Moreover, art performance behearsal time ought be more than movie performance rehearsal time, if they hope to perform the most effective result. Hence, art performance market, it still have these strengths to win movie audience individal leisure choice in global art performance theatre market.

Movie and opera art performance leisure consumer psychology

What does theatre leisure ? Why we need to enter theatre to see movies or enter opera art performance hall to see opera art performance ? Theatre is a place where one group of people- on stage- tell stories to another group of people who are sitting... usually in an auditorium... usually in the dark... listening to, and watching these stories.Since human beings started to gather in groups and communities, they sensed the necessity to transmit their experiences and knowledge- fundamentally- through storytelling. The transmission of these stories, through the ages moved from shamanism to modern forms of art on and off stage.

Theatre is a tool that has existed for thousands of years. I imagine that from the first moments people wanted to transmit their experiences of the hunt, or their father and grandfather. It is both the wish and necessity of human beings to tell stories.Theatre is an art form that brings people together to celebrate, challenge and provoke through the telling of stories. Theatre is unique, you see transformation right in front of you- created in the moment. In a book; you pick it up, put it down and it remains – similarly with film- but with theatre, what you witness in any given moment is unique and only you and the audience will ever experience that.Theatre is a moment of intersection between people where events collide or reveal conflict through storytelling. It is an art-form that always has, and always will be, important and relevant.Theatre is a sense of escape, it transforms you into a new space. It can however, be many things. Theatre can be a source of intellectual learning, inspiration, and can even reflect your life.Theatre is live, and that's important. So much of our art is consumed through live-streams, through computers and so on – and this misses that extraordinary atmosphere, and sense of grounding and presence that theatre gives.

Why do we need to see opera art performance? Going in front of an audience- be it small or large- is a performance?you have to captivate people with what you say, do or whatever! This is the basic of performance.Not everyone can perform. The people who do it have a virtue that they can exploit to get that attention from people. Performance is about having the capability to captivate an audience with whatever means you can see with words, theatre, dance, music and so on.

What does leisure consumer behavior? How to persuade leisure consumer individual feels to enjoy the kind of leisure activities? I shall attempt to indicate art opera performance or movie lesiure example to explain how to persuade audiences feel leisure enjoyment to see the movie or see the opera art performance. For movie or art performance leisure, instead the movie or opera art performance, the artors individual performance attitude whether they can attract any audiences that they can feel enjoyment or leisure seeing feeling and the movie or art opera performance content whether they can attract their leisure emotion factor, the movie and opera art performance whole length of time factor is also important because if the movie or opera art performance time is too long, e.g. above two hours, then the long time movie or opera art performance can not persuade audiences to feel attractive, otherwise, they will feel boring when they feel that they need to sit more than two hours time to see the movie or see the art opera performance in the cinema or art opera performance hall. Unless, the audiences feel very enjoyment to see the movie or art opera performance.So, it explains why general movie or opera art performance time can not exceed two hours. Because instead of performance cost reason, audience individual boring feeling reason is another important audience leisure psychological factor to influence whether the movie or opera art performance can attract or persuade many audiences to choose to to buy ticket to see the movie or the art opera performance.

CINEMA MOVIE AUDIENCE LEISURE PSYCHOLOGY

Theatre is a collaborative art-form with writers, producers, directors, lighting designers, costume makers and so on. When all those pieces coincide, and when the performances are great, the lighting is great, the music is great, the design is great.... when all those different creative activities fuse into one emotional and intellectual delivery- that's when great theatre occurs.

Different films need to arrange different audience individual leisure taste to adapt their seeing movies or opera art performances raising enjoyment feeling.Each year a small number of new release films, 6-10 titles, become 'events'. These films such as the new James Bond, the latest Disney family feature and other big action titles such as the Marvel films or 'sagas' such as Twilight and The Hunger Games, are the bedrock of commercial cinema. These are mass appeal films created at huge cost and supported by massive marketing effort. They provide a disproportionately large amount of a cinema's annual income and they generally appeal strongly to the youth audience (16-24 year olds). 'Event' films are shown widely at multiplex cinemas but often perform poorly in local independent cinemas when shown a few weeks after the initial high profile release although some people will be prepared to wait if they have seen the film trailered at a favourite cinema.

In contrast a large number of high quality, independent and foreign language films are released annually but invariably they earn much less at the box office. These films appeal more to 30+ year olds and can prove to be very popular with particular audiences in individual cinemas. However,in recent years the 45+ age group has become one of the largest growth markets in UK cinemas with films such as The Best Exotic Marigold Hotel with more mature characters and strong storylines aimed at a multi-generational market. Young people, although still the multiplexes mainstay audience, are increasingly consuming film online through downloading or streaming services.

In fact, films based on literary works or specific aspects of social history or parts of the country are often well received by local audiences who prefer cinemas with comfort, character and the opportunity to have a coffee or a bar drink.Young children enjoy cinema going. Sometimes they attend with a group of friends. Often they are accompanied by parents or relatives. Films for the younger age groups are important for local cinemas and may attract sell-out audiences for morning or matinée performances, especially at weekends and during school holidays. Many cinemas now have a regular slot for this audience and operate it like a 'club' to encourage repeated visits. Local cinemas have to be capable of adapting to whatever is currently in the news and available to them. This requires skill and showmanship on the part of the cinema manager and staff in addition to a well designed building.

Why has theatre become such an important art-form?

In my imagination this goes back to the time when we lived in caves. I'm pretty convinced that two people, three people or one person sat on one side of a fire, providing the lighting- while a lot of other people sat on the other side of the cave or dwelling... and from time immemorial stories were told by one or several people, to a larger group of people. These stories may have been history, myths or legend.... they may even have been about religion or about grappling with the seasons.

Stories have always been told by live human beings to other live human beings, that's what makes it such an important and enduring form of art in my view.The unique selling proposition of theatre is the fact that there are live humans in a space, speaking to other live humans. It's not online, not in a cinema, not on some tablet... it's there. As a member of the audience, you are in the same space as the people who are- in the broadest sense of the word- telling stories. The very fact that humanity is at the absolute centre of theatre in tangible flesh and blood terms means that there is intrinsic beauty in that art-form because the human form, human voice and human ability to imagine stories (and their repercussions) is the stuff of art!

The aesthetic and beauty of theatre are very subjective. Performance and theatre can take many forms. It may be a play on the street or- as you saw during the early 19th

century- a form of Opera where many forms of art were gathered into a single performance. The aesthetic of the elements of a performance when they are brought together depend on the culture of the people receiving it and where the piece itself is performed.The aesthetic and beauty of a piece of theatre lies almost completely in the eyes of the person watching.Theatre doesn't have to be beautiful. Some of the most fantastic and thought-provoking pieces are ugly. There is an aesthetic in the staging and design- which should enhance the stories or design of the production- but it doesn't have to be beautiful. Also, the notion of beauty in the theatre is- as in life- defined by the perspective of the viewer. For me, beauty may be defined by other simplicities... stripping away all the white-noise of circumstances and just focussing on human action. That's where I find moments of beauty in theatre, where those absolutely pristine quiet pin-drop moments occur... where the audience, story and artist collide in a moment of truth. These moments of beauty dig deep into an essence. Hence, we each have our own personal aesthetic- but for me the simplicity of storytelling and the collision of human events is where beauty and aesthetic occur in theatre.Theatre always has, and always will be, important and relevant.

THE PSYCHOLOGY OF PERFORMING ARTS:THEATRE AND HUMAN EXPRESSION

Theatre is an arena in which we can mentally play, acting out our fears and fantasies in an experimental way. It excites new ideas and perspectives and provides us with rehearsal for life. In the broad sense, theatre can be taken as referring to films and TV as well as live theatre - indeed, any sort of entertainment that includes performers and audience (sometimes intertwined in complex ways) and which requires imagination to make it real.

Central to much of theatre is human conflict - the characters struggle to attain their ends against opposition, mostly from other characters. Role-playing puts us into the head of each character in turn, allowing us to see things from their viewpoint. By observing how they deal with their problems, sometimes adaptively, sometimes self-destructively, we learn lessons in how to choose among our own options. An important function of theatre is stimulation. Theatre adds magic and thrills to our mundane lives - whether it be disturbing (tragedy & horror), ridiculous (comedy) or romantic (esp. musicals). Modern civilisation has become overly safe. From time to time we need to rock the boat and test the alarms - to try out novel, challenging experiences and sample danger, albeit within a safe context. Theatre and films give us a chance to rehearse reactions to rare, dreaded occurrences such as rape, earthquake, fire or death of a loved one, helping us to cope with such events should they occur in real life. So, the audience leisure need difference between opera art performance and movie. Movie lesiure audiences visual enjoyment needs are whether the movie content is attractive or/and the or artistes their performance skills are proficient. Otherwise, the opera art performance artistes need have the actual time performance skills, because they need to perform to let their opera art performance audiences to feel visual leisure enjoyment immediate, if they can not persuade their opera art performance audiences feel happy or visual leisure feeling, otherwise, they feel boring when they are seeing their opera art performance immediately. They must decide to leave the opera art performance hall. So, all opera art performance artistes need know every opera art performance audience individual emotion, whether he/she is enjoying or boring when he/she is seeing their opera art performance on the performance hall.

What is the role of spectacle in performing arts?

Spectacle is largely a question of means, but it also brings an accent to a presentation or to the way of doing a show. At the beginning of Cirque, we were just a group of street-performers- not great acrobats, so the spectacle was little! As we went along, we were able to add artificial spectacle which was connected to the performance and enhanced with better acrobats- improving the whole experience. Now it would be very hard to go back to 1984 where we were just street-acrobats, people expect and accept spectacle from our performances now.

What is the role of the actor in theatre?

The actor is the person who tells someone else's story, he is the messenger of the story; regardless of whether that story was written by a composer, a lyricist or an author. He is the human-conduit to convey the story to the audience. His or her choices are therefore crucial in making that story as vivid as it can be. Also, the performer and his performance are the skeleton of our production. We can put muscles over this in the form of costumes and lights... we will add music, light and invoke the emotion of this skeleton by bringing it to life, but the performance is at the centre of all of this. Moreover, actors are communicators, storytellers, inventors and commentators. They have many roles in their art, depending on the story they are telling and the genre of the play. Actors are there to entertain, but also to deliver the story as the writer (or they, themselves) would want.As an actor, you are an artist. Greatness comes from the quality of the transformation, experience and how they can access and communicate emotion to effect a change in the audience.

Hence, theatre is an art-form that is meant to be heard. It is a collection of words and moments that are defined by the writer, but ultimately given voice by the actor. For me while it's always story first; the actor is the instrument for those stories coming to life. We each have our own notion of truth, but the great actors are the ones who make truth the through-line of their work. They are the ones who make the boundary between actor and character invisible- immersing themselves in the story. They are the ones who allow the audience to do the same. A great performance is not full of noise, but full of context and story. The actor must be generous, and give with abandon. Real theatre and real performance exists when you have a meeting of the performer and the audience as receiver. The audience are an active participant, theatre is a relationship between the production and the audience- audiences are not just consuming. For example, a piece of theatre is not complete until the audience is in the room. The work is changed by the presence of an audience. When you are making work you see rehearsals and so forth, but what the piece becomes when an audience joins the process translates it to another stage. Whether the audience know it or not, they are active in the process. They clarify things, deny things, join with ideas and more. Moreover, the audience are not passive consumers of theatre, it is a circular relationship.It is extremely important that an audience and a story become one. You often hear people describe the experience of 'losing themselves' in the story; I- personally- would call it 'finding yourself'. My guess would be that if you talk to the average audience member or artist, those unique moments that keep us coming back to theatre are relatively rare; yet we keep going. We want that moment where we get so immersed.. where all the people in the audience and the production come together... that is what resonates with us for years to come.

Designing a Good Theater to influence audience seeing movie or opera art performance positive emotion feeling factor

Instead of learning how to produce one good movie or opera art performance content and the artor individence performance skill and length of performance time arrangement factors, the designing a Good theater location factor will be one important factor to influence audience individual emotion. They may include as below:

Since humanity started gathering to tell stories and represent scenes from everyday life in front of an audience, the need for a space to perform such activities began to increase. Theater design developed from the open-air amphitheaters of the Greeks and Romans to the incredible array of forms we see today. Though some forms work better for particular types of performance, there is no ideal shape or size of a theater. The choice of the best form and scale depends on the functional purpose (movies, lectures, stage performances, musical presentations), the size of the staging required and the number of the audience to be accommodated. Let's see which are the basic parts that comprise a theater and the most common types of today's theater design.

1. Design a functioning Auditorium according to the type of performance and the number of the audience

It is the part of the theater accommodating the audience during the performance, sometimes known as the "house". The house can also refer to an area that is not considered playing space or backstage area. This includes the lobby, coat check, ticket counters, and restroom. The amount of space required for each auditorium depends on a number of factors but the following guides, based on modern seating design can give you an idea of the area needed

2. Keep the standard distance for a comfortable audience seating

The aisle is the space for walking with rows of seats on both sides or with rows of seats on one side and a wall on the other. In order to improve safety when the theaters are darkened during the performance, the edges of the aisles are marked with a row of small lights

3. The stage is important: choose wisely

The stage is the designated space where actors and other artists perform and the focal point for the audience. As an architectural feature, the stage may consist of a platform (often raised) or series of platforms. In some cases, these may be temporary or adjustable but in theaters and other buildings devoted to such productions, the stage is often a permanent feature. There are several types of stages that vary as to the usage and the relation of the audience to them:

Thrust theater stage :

A Stage surrounded by audience on three sides. The Fourth side serves as the background. In a typical modern arrangement: the stage is often a square or rectangular playing area, usually raised, surrounded by raked seating. Other shapes are possible; Shakespeare's Globe Theatre was a five-sided thrust stage.

For greater intimacy with the audience, go with the Thrust Stage

A thrust stage is one that extends into the audience on three sides and is connected to the backstage area by its upstage end. A thrust has the benefit of greater intimacy between the audience and performers than a proscenium while retaining the utility of a backstage area. The audience in a thrust stage theater may view the stage from three or more sides.

End Stage:

A Thrust stage extended wall to wall, like a thrust stage with audience on just one side, i.e. the front."Backstage" is behind the background wall. There is no real wingspace to the sides, although there may be entrances located there. An example of a modern end stage is a music hall, where the background walls surround the playing space on three sides. Like a thrust stage, scenery serves primarily as background, rather than surrounding the acting space.

Arena Theatre stage:

A central stage surrounded by audience on all sides. The stage area is often raised to improve sightlines.

The Proscenium Stage or End Stage :

It is the most common type of stage and it is also called a picture frame stage. Its primary feature is a large opening, the proscenium arch through which the audience views the performance. The audience directly faces the stage and views only one side of the scene. Often, a stage may extend in front of the proscenium arch which offers additional playing area to the actors. This area is referred to as the apron. Underneath and in front of the apron is sometimes an orchestra pit which is used by musicians during musicals and operas.

Flexible theater stage:

Sometimes called a "Black Box" theater, these stages are often big empty boxes painted black inside. Stage and seating not fixed. Instead, each can be altered to suit the needs of the play or the whim of the director.

Keep your theater flexible

Flexible stage theaters are those that do not establish a fixed relationship between the stage and the house. They can be put into any of the standard theater forms or any of the variations of those. Usually, there is no physical distinction between the stage and the auditorium and the audience is either standing, intermingling with the performance or sitting on the main floor.

Profile Theatres stage:

Often used in "found space" theaters, i.e. theaters made by converted from other spaces. The Audience is often placed on risers to either side of the playing space, with little or no audience on either end of the "stage". Actors are staged in profile to the audience. It is often the most workable option for long, narrow spaces like "store fronts". Scenically, a profile theater is most like an arena stage; some staging as background is possible at ends, which are essentially sides. A non-theatrical form of the profile stage is a basketball arena, if no-one is seated behind the hoops.

Sports Arenas stage :

Sports arenas often serve as venues for Music Concerts. In form they resemble very large arena stage (more accurately the arena stage resembles a sports arena), but with a retangular floorplan. When used for concert, a temporary stage area often is set up as an end-stage at one end of the floor, and the rest of the floor and the stands become the audience. Arenas have their own terminology

Keep the scenery low for better visibility

In the Theater in the round or the Arena Stage Theater, the stage is located in the center of the audience, with the audience members facing it from all sides. The audience is placed close to the action, which provides a feeling of intimacy and involvement. However, this type puts major restrictions on the amount and kind of visual spectacle that can be provided for a performance, because scenery more than a few feet tall will block the audience view of the action taking place onstage.

4. Sound quality is as important as visibility

Although theater performances are a visual medium, poor sound quality will ruin even the better plays. The sound is an area often overlooked but, just as you need good sightlines, you also need good sound-lines. Apart from the obvious comfort and size considerations, External sound insulation (how many times have you heard traffic noise, trains or building works over the soundtrack of the film you are watching?) Internal sound insulation – this is particularly important with multiple screens where a loud soundtrack can leak into the adjoining auditorium.Services and equipment noise control – noises such as air conditioning, lifts, toilets and projection equipment need to be controlled. Acoustics – acoustic design in theaters should be considered from feasibility stage – location, auditorium planning etc. through to final commissioning.

What is theatre's economic role?

Every single independent tourist review that is written about reasons why people should come to the UK and London starts with heritage/royalty and then immediately moves on to theatre.... Specifically theatre.... not the arts, not entertainment, not shopping, not restaurants... the theatre. Alongside the fact that theatre employs many people in many diverse and different jobs, it's also a great regenerator of town-centres. If you speak to any government or local-government official that is trying to regenerate cities and towns further, theatres are at the centre. From time to time I get interviewed by an unnamed newspaper about the death of the West End. I always offer to take the journalist around London in a taxi where I can show them boarded up shops, boarded up offices, boarded

up factories and boarded up pubs.
However, theatre is growing globally, and people want it globally. How the work of theatre develop will be a fascinating blend of cultures, it's an incredible opportunity. We currently have three proposals from Shanghai asking us to build, operate and convert theatres as a central core-magnet to retail, residential and other developments. This is alongside conversations we are having in Korea, Hong Kong and more. Around the world, more theatres are being built now than at any other time in history. Theatre will lose the London and New York concentration. Hamburg, Vienna, Melbourne and Sydney are already great theatre cities. Hong Kong is growing into a great theatre destination too. There is also a huge opportunity across Canada and other territories. I see theatre essentially following an upward trajectory in terms of number of cities and venues.

People worldwide now acknowledge theatre is good for society economically and socially.

What does the next 50 years hold for theatre or opera art performance leisure need ? I think the essential core of theatre.... the unique selling proposition of being there to see it, having to perform in a space... will remain the same.... However what that core is saying and doing will depend on the message and story of the artists of the future. The activity of theatre has lasted for many thousands of years. As long as human beings have the need to hear stories, and to tell stories, it will remain. We're in very difficult times at the moment in terms of funding. This does however mean that we tend to get better at what we do. The work gets tougher, leaner and better. I would hope however that regional-theatre funding improves in the future, and we're left with a secure theatre network.

In fact, Theatre is ultimately about conflict between people and circumstances... you can wrap it in a different package and bow, but these principles have remained the same for hundreds of years.In the off-Broadway scene of the 1960s, you saw a trend of self-generating theatre in store-fronts and unusual venues. They were still going after the essence of theatre, but taking it everywhere. If you look today at the influence of technology in theatre, we are now able to do some of the things we used to do by hand- but more easily... for example, throwing a light cue by computer rather than moving dimmers by hand. However, technology gives us more tools to get to the core event, but ultimately the fierce passion the artist has to reveal the story is what powers the theatre.

How do artists cope with the mental pressures of perfection?

I would contest that we all have one or two 'issues' with our mental health, perhaps that is just the normal being of being a human. The discipline of ballet gives you the ability to manage your emotions, and an outlet for them. Ballet is a way to go through your emotions with the permission to exploit your frustrations, investigating them, using them and exposing them.Society faces dangers when people have doubts and questions, and cannot investigate them. When people hold-on to their emotions, and don't become malleable to them.. they become fragile, and can break, like glass.

What is the role of digital technology , how it can influence audience emotion from online movie or opera art performance online watching channel in the modern world?

Digital technology is making us insular. We think we have relationships through Facebook, Twitter and Instagram, but they are not real. There is no physical connection. We are human, we need physical connection. Participating in public performance, where you are a part of something with other people is more important than ever. It's more important than ever that we encourage young people into the arts in a meaningful way where they feel they want to go, and can afford to go. Right now, we can't even get young people through the door- and that's hard.

Looking even further to the future, we are entering the world of artificial intelligence and robotics. There is a chance that machines will be performing many of our world's most physical tasks. Wouldn't it be better if we guarantee the future of our children with creativity? That's the one thing machines can't compete with us on. Human beings will live maybe 100 years, and we leave school when we're 16, 17, 18. We need to teach kids to enjoy learning, to be curious, and to always want to learn. Not one iota of what they will become can be taught by us. The most important thing is that children enjoy the process of discovery. The more we encourage creativity, the more digital technology encourage young age audience group to imagine alternate realities when they can see movie or opera art performance from internet channel, the more our futures will all be brighter.

How has art changed your world-view?

Art has changed my world-view completely. I have travelled the world, not for tourism but to work. I have worked with so many different people, from so many different cultures and backgrounds and I have had my mind opened about humanity.I don't feel that I am a particular person from a particular part of the world. I was born somewhere, grew-up somewhere else, and lived in a few more places. I am a person of the world. Art has allowed me to live with myself, and to make sense of the fragility of humanity's desires and traits. I'm just a human being, and art has given me the space to be OK with that.

What inspires you as an artist? How you are as artist , you feel you may perform your movie or opera art performance to attract audience attention? Working with choreographers and producing stuff that really makes people think, and changes their ideas, and takes them to another place... that's powerful for me. for dance performance example, dance in itself is a social skill that everybody should appreciate and enjoy, our bodies are made to move. If you choose to specialise in the field- you're like an athlete. You have to be built for the technique. The role of the body is important and for dancers, it's about the joints, flexibility and muscular strength. The proportions of the body are also important; that's part of the aesthetic, and you can't help that- this is a visual art. How would be your art performance message to the next generation? You really have to devote your life to theatre. It doesn't mean you can't have a family and so forth... but it isn't like some activities in life where you can get a healthy work-life balance, as much as we would like to encourage it. Theatre is your life as well as your work, and if that doesn't fit with you, then theatre isn't right for you. Whatever your talent... music, movement, whatever... if you have the drive to continue and develop and become a great performer then you should. It's a lot of work- my father used to tell me that in life you need a little bit of talent, but lots of hard work. If you have a little talent, prepare yourself for hard work to develop it, and you may attain greatness; but don't forget that the road to greatness is long. You should make the work that tells the stories you feel are important to you and your generation. The role of a theatre maker is to tell the stories of our lives. You should try and grab the whole of the gamut of emotions, it's not just to entertain. The mix and bravery by which you grab those emotions makes theatre exciting. Moreover, you must be fearless and brave. You must be willing to express what you feel, and to do that with thought. People have a fear of expression, and we must encourage them to do the hard, hard work it takes to overcome this and know they are empowered to make work. All great work comes from this principle, new forms are made, new theatre is created.... When someone stops to write... or stops to raise some money? those are the moments where greatness is created. Also, you have to be curious and learn as much as you can from as many people as you can. You can even learn from people who don't know what they're doing; at least you will then know how not to do something. You have to be kind to yourself. You do not have to suffer or punish yourself to be a great artist. The sooner you can accept yourself, the sooner you can progress and discover what you're capable of. Life is so short, and goes so fast, you have to enjoy it. Life will throw you in so many directions, and goals are not the end; they are simply gateways to more questions, and this process of discovering answers and new questions is never complete, that's life. People have a lot of inhibitions, and are hugely preoccupied with what other people are thinking. Dance gives you a space to forget that, and enjoy being you. I always think you should dance with others, but it's amazing how happy you can be dancing on your own. For me however, the entertainment and enjoyment is dancing with friends or even strangers. Dancing breaks-down so many barriers, and makes you more comfortable with people around you. People let their guard-down when they dance, and it opens a lot of doors for communications.

I have a fitness and dance programme that we take into state-schools. We let kids try anything they want in dance and let their creativity flow. They can do any genre from around the world- the aim is to find something that they can connect with to give them a feel of what dance can do. When you see the reaction? My God, it's the happiest they've ever been! They're testing their bodies like they've never done before, and finding skills that they didn't think they had. It gives them a space to enjoy being themselves, without peer-pressure, without the stresses that can impact their lives so negatively at this early stage.

However, art is one of the most valuable assets of human society, yet the truth is that while we may attach art to a time and a place; it's true provenance and relevance remain intangible. We can look at the raw materials (the paint, the instrument?, the composition (the brush strokes, the music) or even the act of consumption (viewing, listing? – but the thing that we observe only becomes art within us. The phenomenon of art emerges within the intangible mix of experience and cultural inputs that create our mind. A fact not lost on the ancient Greeks who simultaneously originated the concepts of philosophy (the love of wisdom) and theatre (the place for viewing) c.6th century B.C.

The images of other arts are constituted in quite different ways. This engagement has a metaphysical aspect in that the image between the performer and the audience adds up to more than the sum of its various parts. A materialist criticism that does not recognise these 'metaphysical' qualities of theatre is lacking critical force. For the 'beyond physical', the numinous, the spirit, the aura of art, however it is described is a material response to art not just ideological or 'imagined'. This 'something more' than the thing itself is attested to by too many people without deference to gender, race or class. And to ignore it, as though it will go away, and leave us with the quantified, the material and the manipulable, in the name of dogmatic sectarian objectives, is to impoverish the terms on which theatre might be most valuably and pleasurably thought and practiced. This metaphysics of theatre is what is not seen, beyond the practiced, beyond the mind's eye it remains unwritten. It is the domain which both makes theatre worthwhile and simultaneously jeopardises its effects. For it is in this hinterland of the undocumented and discreet that the fallacies of theatre are nourished. This 'something more' of the image does not disconnect the experience of theatre from its place of performance, nor from the everyday. Theatre remains bound by its context precisely through the unique relationship images create between audience, performer and everyday life." He adds that, "To value theatre, is to value life, not to escape from it. The everyday is at once the most habitual and demanding dimension of life which theatre has most responsibility to. Theatre does not tease people out of their everyday lives like other expressions of wish fulfilment but reminds them who they are and what is worth living and changing in their lives every day." (Theatre and Every Day Life, 1993)

The concept of everyday life here is critical. Human beings are cursed with the knowledge of agency. We know without a shadow of a doubt that our immediate experiences are limited simply to ourselves. In many philosophies this is even manifest as the discussion of how one is trapped in the body- able to only experience the substantive world which we have ingested through our limited senses. With this in mind, we quickly see the real power of theatre. Prof. Erin Hurley describes how, "Theatre allows for and offers vicarious experience: the experience of someone else experiencing something?We know that witnessing another's actions and emotional experiences can create the same neurological imprint as doing or feeling them oneself. Joseph Roach provocatively recasts the history of theatre in terms of the good of what he calls 'synthetic experience', a cognate to vicarious experience. The theatre is a port of entry into another's life and another kind of living." (Theatre and Feeling, 2010)

On conclusion, art is the medium by which we- as human beings- are able to relate to each other. Art allows us to understand things that are more than ourselves, and imagine life through the agency of others. Theatre- as perhaps the most human of all the arts- has the profound ability to engage us immediately in the experience of someone else's agency- at any point in time, at any place. It breaks down the loneliness of being a self, and allows one to realise that not only are there others- but that the self can be them too. Art Business Charity conflict creativity culture. So, any movie or opera art performance businessmen need to educate our next generation needs to considerate art performance movie or opera art performance lesisure industry needs to be continued to develop in order to let they can learn more new art culture and build positive charter role in our society, then crimes number will be influenced to reduce when they can see any health movie or opera art performance after they buy tickets to enter cinemas or opera art performance hall and let they feel that it is valuable economic spending time to see the movie or the opera art leisure performance.